The Longest Labor

Reflections On Being Open To Life, And The Beautiful Vocation Of Motherhood

REBECCA MACK

TilmaRose Press: TilmaRosePress@Protonmail.com

Book design & graphic by Rebecca Mack

Cover art by Rachel Fifelski (www.rachelfifelskiart.com)

The Longest Labor/Rebecca Mack - 1st ed.

ISBN (paperback): 978-0-578-38178-7

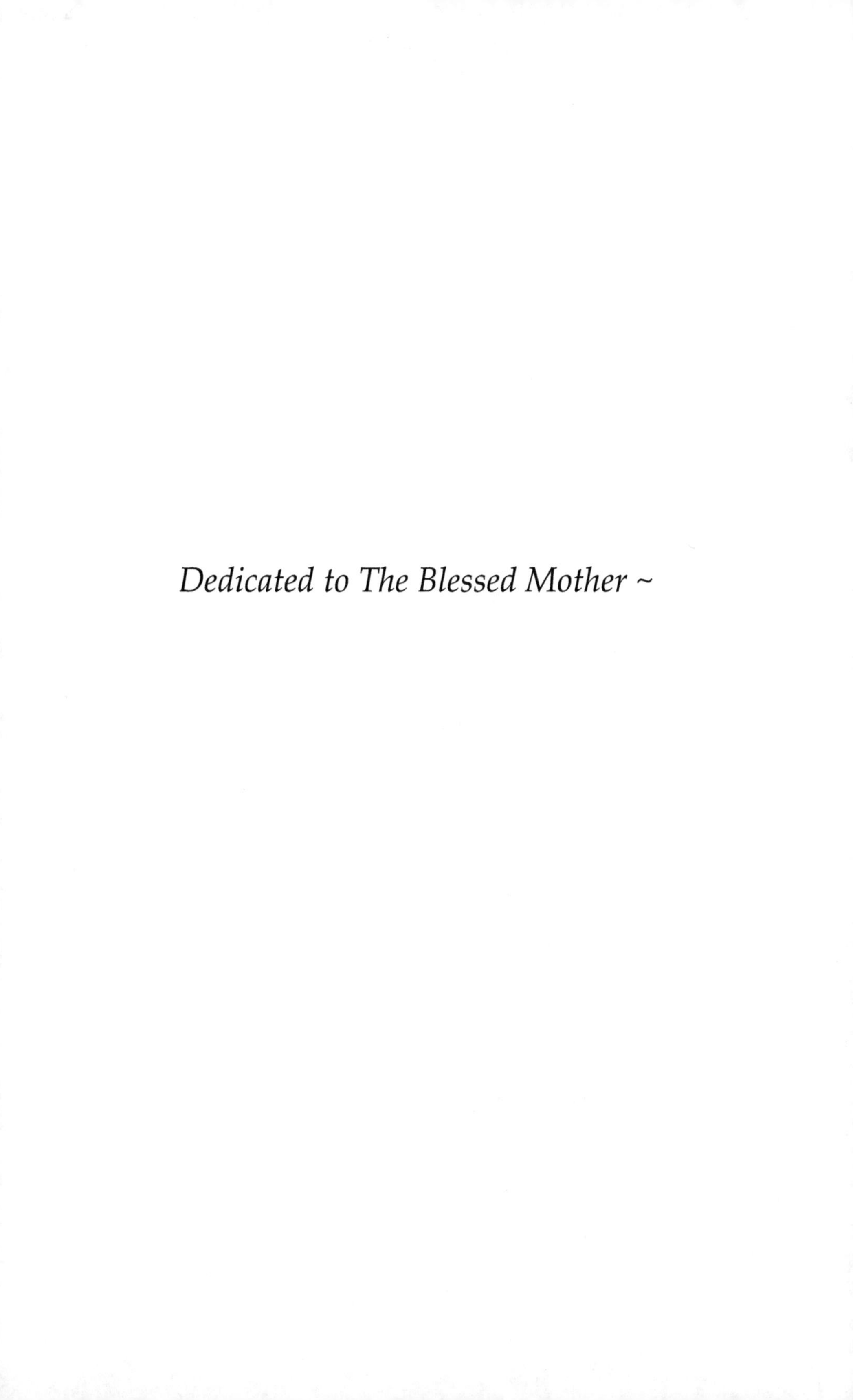

Dedicated to The Blessed Mother ~

Table of Contents

The Longest Labor

Introduction

The loveliest masterpiece of the heart of God is the heart of a mother. ~St. Therese of Lisieux

Labor, as in bringing forth a child from its mother's womb, usually finds us in the care and encouragement of another - or others - who usher us into motherhood, whether it be for the very first time, or for the tenth time and beyond. The support from our husband, midwife, doula, OB, or nurse lends a stability and strength to our feat which we might not have known otherwise. So, too, do we find ourselves aching for this support throughout our vocation of motherhood, and in life. There are many reasons behind my putting ink to paper on this topic of motherhood. The main reason, and the focus of this particular work, is to give support to those of you who are in the midst of this rewarding, yet daunting, vocation of motherhood. It is my hope that this book will not only serve as that support, but it will also encourage any of you who are reluctant to let go and let God take control.

In having met, spoken with, confided in, sought counsel from, and in counseling other women myself, I have found the collective longing for a community of like-minded women: women who are open to life not just once or twice, but as many times as God wills. These women's lifelong labors extend far beyond the years society has deemed acceptable for bearing and raising children, and their hearts are open to children, to their vocation, for an indefinite time frame, claiming all the graces abounding therein.

I will be the first to admit that this is not always an easy thing to do. It is hard to put aside - or at the very least, not always have time and energy to pour ourselves into - our creative sides: the other parts of us that are not about children, husbands, and household responsibilities. It is difficult to know we are, or could be, really good at something out in the world that does not involve diapers, dishes, laundry or nursing. But we choose to give it up, or put it on hold, because we desire to put *all* of our main focus on raising our families. I realize that there are women who have found ways to balance their time and talents between work and family. My musings are not a slight against them. However, support seems to be less and less available for those of us who choose to live a more traditional lifestyle, focusing mainly on our family and home life and not wishing for anything different. In fact, it seems there is a collective idea rising within society that there is something wrong with women like us.

If you identify with that last line especially, mama, this book is for you.

My desire is to reach out to those of you who are just starting out, or are stuck on your path; to those who are fearful, and to those who have doubts; to those who are shamed, and to those who find it difficult to grasp even the tiniest bit of hope to continue on in your vocation with joy; or to those who just want a little camaraderie along the way. If you can relate to any one of these descriptions, it is with you that I want to share my thoughts, and offer some encouragement and hope for these long years we will tarry here in this place.

I certainly do not have all of the answers. My longest labor is but seventeen years new, and so far, the Lord has blessed me with twelve babies; three of which were taken back soon after they were conceived. There are certainly more women I know who have much more experience than I, and could probably impart so much more than I can on this subject. But I want to try anyway. I want to *"rejoice with those who rejoice, and weep with those who weep."* With you, I want to sit and ponder the beautiful gift of motherhood, both the joy and the sorrow. Into your heart, I want to dive deep and dwell on the important things in life. I wish to unpack with you this most wondrous vocation, in all of its grit and glory; to walk along with you as, together, we figure out not only how to truly live out this vocation in an authentic, Catholic, and intentional way, but how to bring glory to God in the process.

Motherhood really is the longest labor of our lives, and we should encourage each other through it. Aside from society's anti-life message, there are many reasons why we might hesitate on our journey: difficult marriages, unsupportive families, overwhelming household dynamics, lack of finances, or just plain fear. Within my ramblings herein, I share my thoughts and experiences on several of these topics, with the prayerful desire that you will find, not only empathy and encouragement, but also a message of hope; one which convinces you that above all, God loves you, has a plan for your life, and His will - whether active or passive - is in *every single* moment of it. There truly is nothing to fear. I walk this journey with you as someone who is still learning, (and sometimes relearning!), what it looks like to trust God's love, mercy, and Divine Providence in all things. I am not perfect, and possibly like you, am often feeling a bit lost.

Because this journey through motherhood is a *labor* (of love), you will find that I often parallel it with the actual physical labor we go through to bring forth our children. In doing so, I hope to impart an understanding that this longest labor only *begins* with an offering of our bodies as a haven for a growing baby, and then a process to birth; both short-lived. But it continues as a call to a lifetime of servanthood and sacrifice that brings glory to God. In addition, we are hopefully raising future saints who will one day make it to Heaven to glorify Him for all eternity! The journey is long and arduous, but not without joy and reward. When we seek to give our entire lives to the King of Kings, including our family size, we are blessed beyond measure, and our souls magnify His goodness to the world. Though it may seem that we are few and far between, there are some of us still left in the world ready to accompany you during your longest labor; ready to offer an ear, a shoulder, our love, and our hearts.

Here is mine.

Writing Babies into Existence

Children are a gift from the Lord, the fruit of the womb, a reward. Like arrows in the hand of a warrior are the children born in one's youth. Blessed are they whose quivers are full.
~Psalm 127: 3-5

As a writer, there is nothing more terrifying, yet exciting to me, than a blinking cursor against the backdrop of a stark-white blank screen. Nothing, except giving birth to a baby. And actually, there is nothing more terrifying, yet exciting to me, than giving birth to a baby...except raising one; or in my case, many.

The fear component is one of great magnitude. Not in the laboring itself, but in that which has been placed into our trembling hands: a baby. And not *just* a baby, but with it, the responsibility of ushering that baby through this life, and doing so *well*. Sometimes, the fear overwhelms us to the point of deciding we never want to do *this* again. And yet, we don't remember. We don't want to recall. We forget. Time passes, another babe comes, and we find that we forgot that terror, that paralyzing fear that crept up on us somewhere in between contraction one and baby delivered. Do you know that fear? It's the one that tells us this will be the *longest labor* of our life. The longest one. It dares to ask us: are we ready?

The truth is, no one is ready to raise a child. No one is ready to raise two children, or three. Or more. Especially not in the culture we live in today. Let's face it: society as a whole doesn't exactly hold children in high regard. Truth be told, it hasn't for many decades. It is especially not very accepting of those of us who choose to allow the Creator of Heaven and Earth to also create new life within us as many times as He wills. Those of you with big families know that we are pretty much looked upon as a circus side-show these days. After two or three children, we are already put into a category all our own. (I think the label is, 'freaks.') The world taunts us, begging these questions - How in the world will we afford all of those kids along with a big, fancy house and several cars between us, vacations thrice a year and dining out every weekend? How else will we be able to do whatever we want if we have more than the allotted number of children whom we can't wait to help grow up and scoot out the door so we can get back to *really* living?

Having children and being a stay-at-home mom, regardless of the number of kids, is a tough feat these days. But I've often wondered why it feels so much more difficult than it was even when I first started out seventeen years ago. Is it because our culture has turned even more away from a culture of life? Are there more people less concerned about raising Godly children and more people concerned about the number of children others have? In the daily 'pursuit of happiness', have we forgotten what happiness actually looks like? Something else? I think that as society has gone to a more self-centered and Godless approach to life, we have lost an essential component of what it means to be a community, which is to encourage and support each other in our human existence.

What is interesting about this is, that while there is a collective lack of support, there is plenty of willingness to criticize. Since Eve's journey into the land of motherhood, women have been bearing and raising children like nobody's business. And it isn't anyone's business. It isn't anyone's business when you're expecting number six even though you just had number five less than two years ago. It isn't anyone's business that you're going forth, being fruitful and multiplying, at all, really.

There is this deception in which our culture is currently entrenched. It is that babies are a commodity, and that their value is based on whether or not they are wanted; if we have room for them in our neat little pre-planned lives. This broken way of thinking is why we get such a negative response from people when we announce the blessing of another baby. Sometimes, this happens within our own families, and even within our own parishes. People believe it's their business what our families look like, and the pain they cause with their words and lack of support often weighs heavily on our hearts.

It's a lonely life we live sometimes, isn't it? As a very young mother, I wanted all the support I could get, and not finding it in certain people within our family was devastating. Coupled with the fact that I had a huge problem with caring what people think of me, it was a painful road to travel; especially when I expected joy, and instead, found anger or sorrow directed toward us over the news of another baby's existence. This was not found only within our family. Friends, and also strangers, felt the need to give their opinions. When we were a young family with four small children, a woman, with whom I thought I was becoming friends, made some rude comments to another woman about the size of our family. At that time, I was also watching two little girls for a man who had lost his wife in a car accident. This woman just couldn't understand why, or even how, I could be open to having "so many" babies of my own, as well as care for two who were not mine. Needless to say, it was very difficult for me to make eye contact with her for a long time after that.

Years of these types of experiences wear on a woman. When I found myself pregnant with my fifth, I was so worried about what others would say, I couldn't even enjoy that positive pregnancy test. Think about that for a moment.

There I was, having been given once more the miracle of bearing within me another living soul to raise for God's glory, and all I could think about was other people's thoughts on the matter. The most painful aspect of that moment was the fact that the year prior, I had lost a baby. I grieved for a long time. Yet even when we were given the chance to have another one, I allowed the nay-sayers to be the voice in my head. They were so effective that I allowed my joy to be stolen at a time when it should have been especially strong in light of the previous loss.

The fault here is mine, however. I should not have allowed it to be that way. I should have been stronger in my faith, my beliefs, and my humility. The truth is, we all have to learn to get to a point where the only opinion that matters to us is God's. In the way we live our lives as a family, in the way we choose to raise our children, all that matters is what God thinks. The not-so-secret to this is that, if we are following what He says to do and prayerfully discerning His path for our life, receiving the sacraments and following actual Church teachings, we already know what He thinks. I try to remember that people come and go (unfortunately this includes family as well as friends), but the Lord is ever-present, and our life on this earth is actually to be lived for Heaven. So, if we are too worried about what other people think, and we are making decisions based on that, those decisions are drawing us away from our path to Heaven, and we are failing.

I sometimes think about my experiences with people who would often make comments or encourage a different way of living than we chose. I used to just want things to be easy, so in order to avoid conflict within these relationships, I would actually start to consider what they said. But then I would think, "Is this, at the end of my life, going to award me that, '*well done, my good and faithful servant*' from my Lord, or is it going to lead to so many more answers I will have to give for my failure to do His will?"

Even still, I found myself a little anxious when, not too long after my fifth child was born, I knew there would definitely be a sixth. Not just that it was a possibility, but deep down in my heart, I somehow *knew* my womb would definitely be opened once more and God would write yet another baby into existence. In that quiet, secret place, another tiny life would be knitted, ever so gently, into the fabric of our family's life. And while I wasn't sure I could handle another one, somehow, the knowledge that she was already written into the story had made its indelible mark. Life was difficult, yes. So much more difficult than I ever imagined it would be. But there was no question, the Lord had placed it upon my heart that there would definitely be yet another babe. And I had to decide: will I angst about this, pouring over all the what-ifs, can't-dos, and the shouldn'tbes, or will I trust that the Lord, Who knows all things, knows what He is doing, even with my messy, sometimes hesitant, fiat?

I'd like to say I didn't angst at all after that moment of clarity, but the fact is, despite my faith, despite my knowing how much He loves me and is taking care of me, I still worry sometimes. But I have come to realize that it's okay to feel worried. Worry is a very real emotion. But when we take our worries and place them at the foot of His cross, when our deepest desire is to conform to His perfect and holy will, when we trust in Him, He gives us the strength to take up our crosses and to have peace and joy while carrying them. Maybe not peace at every *single* moment, but often. Time and time again, we turn to Him, we cry out, we surrender, and He lifts us up.

In Fr. Lovasik's, *The Catholic Family Handbook,* he writes, *"If your large family brings ridicule from neighbors and even strangers, remember that you have a lasting treasure worth suffering for, and that the Lord called blessed those who suffer persecution for justice's sake." A treasure worth suffering for.* Remember that! Remember, in those moments which often smite our motherly hearts, we are put into a very humbling position of suffering, which will bless us immensely if we allow it.

When I look back on those younger years of my life as a mother, I have a better understanding of the bigger picture. I now see how far-reaching the harm is that negative attitudes can cause. These negative attitudes are ever-growing in prevalence, even in Catholic parishes, and serve only to harm the Church as a whole. I cannot even tell you how many Catholic women I have spoken with who fear the possibility of having more than two or three children for the *sole* reason of knowing they will get backlash and lack of support from their families and people in their parish community. It is a shame, and also astounding, to realize that this is becoming more and more mainstream: families, friends, an entire society, who shames others over their family size. But forgive! Pray for those who hurt you in these situations! They truly do not know the depths of their error.

Believe me, I know how very important it is to have that support; most especially within our parishes and faith life. It can be challenging to be a member of a church where there are very few large families and the general attitude toward large families is negativity. An atmosphere like that is not conducive to being nurtured, encouraged, or supported to walk a path of faith that adheres to the wisdom and teachings of Holy Mother Church. It makes it easier to fall. It makes it easier to stray. My own family was in an environment like that, and it was difficult. But, after years of prayer, we were called to a more traditional church family whose members try to live out their daily life steeped in the Catholic Faith and all of Her teachings, including being open to new life in accordance with God's will. It is an amazing blessing, and we are so grateful to the Lord for hearing our humble prayers and gifting us an environment that will help us to grow ever-closer to Him through the fullness of His truth, found in the depth and beauty of our Catholic faith.

And now, I watch my number six gallivanting through the house with her siblings. The curls that I long-awaited through much of her first two, mostly-bald years, bounce against her slender neck, her giggles echo through the halls like a symphony played just for my heart. Her bright, hazel-brown eyes light up as she grabs my face and smothers me with kisses, or while she holds her brother's hand or snuggles close to her sisters. And I think - *this soul who has filled our home with so much love and wonder, has always been here. She has always been part of us, because that is what God willed.* As her mother whose womb is where she was so carefully and lovingly knit seven years ago, I thank God that I said yes to that Will, despite my misgivings, despite my hardships, despite my selfishness and pride. Despite what anyone else thought, I said yes.

I feel a sense of gratitude every time I look at her. For she is the one I dared to accept. She is the one who materialized the reality that our fears don't have to be at odds with our beliefs. We can get beyond any fear on the wings of understanding that this path is for our good, because He works all things for good. The Father of the entire universe writes each of our lives with His perfect pen and ink blotter. He writes our stories with room for all of their gory and glorious details; with room for every pain and smatter of ugliness, and every joy-filled morning and permeating sunset. He pencils in space for all our fears, our joys, our laughter, and our tears. And yes, He writes even every baby. *Every* baby. He writes them all into existence. And sometimes, sadly, He writes them back out. But *He* is the author of all life. And His story never ends.

Laboring Through the Story

The special power of loving that belongs to a woman is seen most clearly when she becomes a mother. ~St. Teresa of Calcutta

In the natural birthing world, they say you should write down your birth story shortly after it happens. It's an exercise in remembering, recording, filling up, letting go. They say to write it all down, even the details you don't think really need to be written. In a few years, you will have forgotten. In a few years, you will have very little recollection of what transpired on that day, in those moments when your body and nature and God's perfect will worked together to bring forth your child. Those details will be replaced with the tickling of chubby knees at bath time, or the sound of erratic giggles as you chase your toddler through the house. You won't remember the painful need to push them out, but the aching impossibility of keeping them in... keeping them with you; not letting them grow up.

I didn't write my birth stories right away. Not any of them. In fact, I have a couple I still haven't taken the time to think about more deeply in order to write them down. I forgot. I didn't think I would, but I did. It's like when you wake in the middle of the night with a deep thought or a seemingly fantastic idea blaring in your mind, and you tell yourself you'll remember it in the morning, because you're too tired to get up and find a piece of paper to write it down. And let's face it, this has happened a thousand times before, so you have paper by your bedside, but you're just too lazy to roll over, put on your glasses and write it down. You'll remember, you tell yourself; in the morning when the sun is awake and you're not so cozy between the sheets. But of course you don't remember. You never do. The thoughts were stolen away in the night, lost in the folds of wandering dreams.

So those last few baby stories of mine have yet to be written. I think, if I sit long enough and really drum my brain a little, I *might* be able to remember them. I will need help from the people who were there, encouraging me, supporting me, helping me usher my baby to this side of the womb. These people include my husband, midwife, and my sister. Just as I needed help from them then, I need help now...to recall...to write down...to release.

I want to share part of the story of my first baby. I think it is important to share that story here. In sharing hers, I share part of mine. I share a part of me that has been both difficult to approach, and long in healing. It is important because it gives a foundation to these last seventeen years or so. It is something tangible to hold on to. Most importantly, it underscores the Lord's promise that all things work for good for those who love Him.

A bitter-cold rain fell that November morning. The birthing room was bathed in a quiet calm. I was tired. We had come to the birthing center in the wee hours of the morning after a long night of laboring at home. My midwife didn't think I was ready to come in, but I begged to anyway, as if going to the birthing center would somehow make my baby come faster. I was young and didn't know what I was doing. We drove thirty minutes in torrential rain, got settled in and walked. And walked. And walked. As the early morning light dawned and slid quietly through the windows, refracting through silvery drops of rain, I continued to walk the floor and the stairs, a thousand rounds, making my way, hoping the baby was making hers.

Eventually, my midwife determined that we should transfer to the hospital. There was no real medical reason, but since she wasn't sure why I wasn't progressing, she felt I should go. Everything turned ugly after that. At the hospital, I was subjected to abuse. I was a victim of the system, and I didn't even realize how bad it was at the time. They say that if you come out with a healthy baby, what else matters? I'll tell you what matters: A LOT. A lot matters. I didn't realize it then, but amidst the receiving blankets and pink-and-blue striped baby hat placed with my belongings, I walked away from that hospital with the baggage of PTSD as well. It would be a long time until I could completely unpack that bag.

Nevertheless, my first born came after over 48 hours of labor, via cesarean. I was pretty out of it from all of the drugs they gave me. I was there, laying behind that plastic sheet they put up so you can't see what's going on, floating on a sailboat amidst sunny waves drawn on the sheet by the anesthesiologist. *Pay no attention to the woman behind the curtain, eh?!* I am pretty sure I felt like my entire body was falling apart with the pressure. Her father held her up announcing that she was a girl. Through the fog, I'm sure I whispered, "I know."

But this, this was not her beginning. I'm a strong advocate for the Truth of life, and the Truth is that life begins *at the moment of conception.* My daughter's story begins there, in that quiet place. In the secret darkness of conception. It begins with the beautiful way God does indeed work all things for good; and how, when we are contrite, this even applies to *sin*. Suffice it to say her dad and I were not married at the time she was conceived. Mistakes were made. But the Lord had something to say, and our sweet daughter came to be.

The moment I found out I was pregnant is one I will never forget. I was a very young, childish, immature twenty-two year-old with a messy life and no clear direction. Late one night, I wandered around a Rite Aid searching for something to purchase with the pregnancy test I had just picked up, as though a tube of mascara or a Twix candy bar could make it less obvious in my young, ringless hands. Even as I set the test down on the bathroom sink back at my townhome, I knew it would be positive. I was afraid of the new life those double pink lines would bring me. Terrified, actually. But as the moments ticked on and the lines grew darker, I became wrapped in a blanket of peace, one I had never known before in my life.

However, that peace, though a constant fixture beneath all of my other emotions throughout my pregnancy, wasn't as tangible to me after that night. Reality has that effect on peace sometimes. Especially back then, my lack of faith put me into a place of both awe and confusion. There was no room for that tangible peace in the midst of the battle I fought within myself. I am convinced that much of what we view as 'surreal' in this life, is really a matter of our minds and spirits at war with each other. Back then, it looked a little something like this:

Fact: I am pregnant, unmarried and young. Fact: I can barely take care of myself. Fact: My family won't raise my child for me. Fantasy: Maybe they will? Fantasy: I could give this baby up and life would be exactly as it was before. Fact: God is perfect. Fact: I've got this, with Him, together.

What's really interesting about that time is that, though her father wanted us to try to have a real relationship and be together for her, I did not want to. I didn't want to, and yet, the Holy Spirit seemed to have different plans. For a while, I researched adoption options. Then, we sought counsel with a priest, who urged us to think about dating properly; and reluctantly, I agreed. He encouraged us to not worry about the baby's future just yet. When I was seven months along, after I had finally come to a place of excited anticipation of a new life with my baby, with or without him, her dad asked me to marry him. I knew just then that this was our path. That same peace that had wrapped itself around my soul the night I found out I was pregnant was there on that bright summer day when he drove me to an overlook in the mountains and asked me to be his wife.

I believe in the power of prayer, and I believe in the supernatural power of God's will. We had choices, yes, and many were wrong, but some of our choices, I believe, were driven by a spirit of God's will that we wanted to follow, even if only subconsciously. So that day he asked me to marry him and I said yes? God's will was made known. I had been fighting for so long against the idea of us being a couple, and even the fact that we had created a baby together hadn't been enough for me to think it was the right choice. Then, all of the sudden, just like that, it was. And it wasn't anything he or I did. We certainly hadn't dated for a very long time. There were still aspects about one another neither of us liked; still much of each other to discover. I'm not a material person so even a sparkling diamond ring glinting in the July sun could not have swayed me. It was the perfect love of Christ manifested in a future we both saw full of promise, hope, and supernatural grace. Now, I'm not saying that I felt the Lord calling me to marry him, but that because we were both open to His plan for our lives, He took our willingness and gave us the graces we needed to see some of the beauty and the possibility in making that choice.

The story of life is made up of many moving parts, each joined together as if on a cog; the movements of any one part consequential to the part beside it. Our choices, our mistakes, our free will, give us the framework to progress with the pull of the supernatural love of God, and His will for us. Within that framework are those parts. But some break, or don't work, or somehow keep us from moving forward. And they are replaced. When we see them for what they are, when we realize they are, in reality, inhibiting us, then the old part is repaired or replaced, and we're once again moving along. If we are steadfast, we reach our proper destination; a new life. Our purpose is fulfilled and the labor of love, complete. I believe that within the events of the beginning of our relationship, I found the strength and foundation to embrace my vocation as a mother. Like in that cog, the three of us became a unit, moving parts working together, her daddy and I changing and rearranging in order to continue on our journey toward the Lord and His will for our lives.

Bringing our baby home from the hospital, I remember feeling like I couldn't love her enough. I already loved her so much, yet I thought it would never be enough. So much had happened to get to that point that, at times, it left me with a sense of inadequacy and incompetence, especially on that very first day. I was conflicted deep within myself. Her daddy and I planned our wedding for just weeks after her birth, and knowing she would be there with us left me with an intense feeling of guilt. I was also reeling from the trauma I experienced at the hospital. Between abusive nurses and a broken system, my psychological health was ravaged. I felt like I was battling between the effects of the trauma and the hormones that had flooded my body upon birth, and life was in an upheaval for a while. Overshadowing that, however, was the excitement of becoming a family and journeying the path that God laid out for us - that love story we began - come hell or high water.

Hell And High Water

Love is the key to the mystery. Love by its very nature is not selfish, but generous. It seeks not its own, but the good of others. The measure of love is not the pleasure it gives - that is the way the world judges it - but the joy and peace it can purchase for others.
~Archbishop Fulton Sheen

One thing you should not do while in labor is fight the waves. Not even as they get progressively bigger and heavier. You have to be willing to work through them. You have to be aware of the enormity of your situation, size up those waves and then, at the right moment, let go and ride them out. Sometimes you'll be able to do this with finesse and sometimes, not. Sometimes you will vocalize your pain from deep within you, if only to reassure yourself that you are still, in fact, alive. But, whether or not you do it with finesse isn't the point. The point is that you do it. You cannot run from the waves of labor; and you should not run from those of life.

The story of my husband and me is a very interesting one. It is interesting and loaded with so many ups and downs, *waves* of beauty, misery, grace. It is one of those types of stories which probably needs more than a simple nod in the midst of a related story to really grasp, especially if you want to understand how amazing the Lord's grace truly is. One of these days, I know I'll write it all down in its entirety. But here I will just impart that nod; a simple glimpse into our life, our marriage, our journey as parents, as it pertains to this story here and now.

I have my husband's permission to say this: the beginning of our marriage was horrendous. In fact, when I say this, he'll dramatically nod in agreement. There would be no hurt feelings, no accusing glares. We know, and fully admit to, the deep cavernous wasteland our marriage was at the start. So when I say horrendous, I definitely mean it. Capital H and everything! HOR.REN.DOUS. But - and here is one of the biggest 'buts' I could probably ever impart to any aspect of my life – the Lord is gracious and merciful. Did you get that? *He is gracious and merciful.* That is simply all there is to it. And it's why we can talk so openly about how horrendous things were at the start. It's why we can even talk about it with a smile. And in talking about it, we hope to encourage others in their own marriages, and give them something that is relatable and inspiring. Truly, marriage isn't called a sacrament for nothing. Grace comes with sacraments. It reminds us that there is something much bigger than 'you and me' and the anger and hurt between us.

Sometimes we have to take a breath; walk away; but come back, and let the grace of God clean up the mess. Oh, how many times did we each want to walk away and not come back!

Speaking for myself, I know there were so many times when the lessons I was learning were completely forgotten when it came time for the test. There were many times that, despite my *knowing* the way I am to show my love, I chose not to anyway. Unfortunately, there are still so many more of those times than I'd like to admit. I try to give myself some slack and remind myself at least it's not as bad as it used to be. But I also don't allow that to be 'good enough;' because he deserves so much better than that, and our children do, too. Honestly, it was hell. The high water came eventually...

It got to the point where, in the middle of our living room, in the midst of our battles, when love seemed all but lost and nothing seemed to make any sense, the water was rising around us. It was rising around us and there was nary a life vest to be seen. We were beginning to drown. It rose above us and lifted us up for a while, but eventually, it got so deep that we got so tired of treading water, and we both started to sink. Several kids into our marriage, several jobs, a big move, so many things had taken place. Though things changed and rearranged around us, and even though we each changed in some ways, the biggest ways were left yet untouched and forgotten, or maybe just kind of ignored.

Oh...and the elephant in the room: neither of us knew how to swim, let alone navigate these waters.

We spent a long time battling each other, and battling ourselves. Despite having one kid, two kids, three kids, more. We grew together then apart; in the same direction, then off on different roads; all the while, trying to figure out how to be good parents, and how the heck were we supposed to raise these children and teach them to know, love and serve God. How were we supposed to instill in them the knowledge of life and love, or even the beauty and wonder in a world we aren't meant for, when we couldn't get our stuff together ourselves? Our eyes were closed. We were blind. We didn't know much about any of those things, at least, not really. The problem with this is that eventually, if you don't get those lessons learned and all your baggage unpacked, the little people to whom you have given life start to suffer. They start to suffer and it also adds to your labor, and in the end, as time moves on and they grow up and go out into the world, it adds to their own as well.

It's interesting to me to look back on that time and really see how little we understood, and how much we consistently chose ourselves over each other or, more importantly, over the Lord. We certainly had enough of a sense of our path to take those first few steps, but it seems like we got distracted a little. Something shiny across the way, a different, seemingly much easier path, perhaps. That peace we felt in choosing each other didn't come with knowing all the things we would be up against. It isn't to say we never should have gotten married in the first place. Some might say that. Perhaps from a worldly perspective it would be true. But despite how awful things were, we clung to the Lord through all of the storms, and with the graces afforded to us, we were made new, and love bloomed. Glory to God!

While most people don't actually *start* a marriage in such a dire state, the truth is, every single marriage has probably gone through some rocky times. How rocky might solely depend on the level of the couple's willingness to work together through them in humility. But there are hardships at some point, nonetheless. My husband and I have been blessed beyond measure by the graces afforded to us by a sacramental marriage, and especially through our continued partaking in the gifts of the Sacraments in general. The utilization of the tools of our Catholic faith, such as confession and Holy Communion, help us to forge on; help us to continue to be willing to work toward the common goal of a Godly union in which our family unit would be not only intact and surviving, but thriving.

Sometimes, we sinful human beings choose to ignore our paths, and when things get tough, instead of utilizing the tools of our faith, we run from them. Fast. And we hide. Because sometimes, the effects of those tools seem to be painful at first. Sometimes, in the heat of moments angry and dark, they sting. They prick at the very center of our hearts, scraping wounds raw and fleshing out our pain. But we have to remember that it is only to allow grace to become the healing balm to such pain. Grace, which is God's life in us, is the cure. Fulton Sheen once said, *"Sometimes the only way the good Lord can get into some hearts is to break them."* It may sound harsh and even allude to a mean God, but if we think about all of the ways in which beautiful things are created, we will recognize the naturally difficult path they journey to get there. It truly is the only way. The way of love. And it is perfect.

Another important tool we have at our disposal is that which is imparted by a good and holy priest - the continual preaching on sin and its effects on our lives. It seems to be that, in these times, many people go to Mass and listen to the sermon and often leave with a lot of 'feels,' and not much conviction. It leaves them with a sense of mediocrity, of contentment, of "good enough." God loves us, yes, He does. We should rejoice in that, of course. But also, we are to love Him. How can we show God that we love Him? By striving to avoid sin. When we listen week after week to sermons that don't reinforce this, that don't convict us of our sin, that don't encourage us to do all that we can to run away from sin, or that don't give us guidance on how to avoid it, we aren't motivated to do so. At least, not so much.

I have noticed a huge difference in our spiritual and family life since we switched church communities to a traditional one. (Of which there are many, by the way. Ours is not exclusive.). By saying I've noticed a big difference in our spiritual life doesn't mean we consider ourselves 'holier than thou.' We acknowledge how truly far we still have left to go in our journey to Heaven. We are not perfect, of course, but we desire to be. We are constantly encouraged to strive for that; to avoid sin, to live our lives as holy, faithful Catholics, which admittedly, was not always a goal we kept in the forefront.

I remember a particular day a few years ago, when my husband and I had a disagreement. He had hurt me with his words and lack of sensitivity, when I felt like I needed him to lift me up and comfort me. That very next day, our priest's sermon was about men loving their wives like Christ loves the Church. It wasn't about 'feeling good', it wasn't sugar-coated or expressed in such a way that appeals to our emotions. It was direct and deep and convicting to our *souls.* My husband's heart was moved and he turned to me in that instant, when we were still struggling to come back to unity, when he was still not inclined to have compassion for me. And, I, too, was moved to let go of my resentment and forgive him.

Another important factor is the strength that freely giving ourselves to each other and being open to life actually bestows upon a marriage. But within that idea, there is a deeper gift. I look back on the births of our babies, the actual physical labor process, and I notice a very important factor in them. That is, despite whatever was going on between us, my husband's efforts to help me along and be a solid support during those long hours was so steady and strong, it was not only observed, but also *felt,* by the rest of my birthing team. He was incredibly attentive to my needs, even in the wee hours of the morning, forsaking sleep and sustenance to not only be present for me, but also to pray for and with me!

I have a memory of my husband, during a particularly intense moment of labor, grabbing hold of my shaking hands, enveloping them within his own steady ones, and praying the *Our Father* aloud, encouraging me to pray with him, to focus on the words, to release my tension to the Lord. He knew I needed that, though I said not a word to him. Words truly fail to describe the connection between us during the labor and delivery of our babies. But I honestly believe that those opportunities to connect and grow in our love have been one of the biggest aspects of our survival. It is one thing to make a baby. It is an entirely different thing to go through the labor process unified as a team, and then go on to raise those sweet, (yet often difficult), blessings together.

Of course, labor is temporary and life goes on. So it does not make all things blissful forever. But with that new-found strength, we move on, we grow, we try. We accept another blessing and we recommit ourselves to our relationship, our parenting, and our path. In the heart of our humble, sometimes-broken home, we gather as a family and pray. Never perfect, always striving. Seventeen years in the trenches of this longest labor has taught me this: you can never go back, only forward, and time does not necessarily heal all wounds. But the grace and mercy of our Lord gives us the courage to rise above the tallest waves, and the strength to *forgive* even the most difficult and painful things. As a result, *His love* heals. When we mirror that, despite our imperfections, love endures.

Love Enduring

Love consists not in feeling great things but in having great detachment and in suffering for the Beloved.
~St. Maximilian Kolbe

There are four stages of labor. The one I like the most is the last stage, (and not just because the pain is all but gone!) That is the time when all the world around you seems to stand still and it's just you and your spouse, and that beautiful new babe, locked inside that bubble of timelessness. What a sacred moment! I realize that the details of this stage vary from birth to birth, and from woman to woman. But for me, with my babies, this stage is the crème de la crème. The waves have subsided some, the prize has been brought forth and instantly there is that enduring love that surmounts all else. And there is that moment when it dawns on you that you have loved her your entire life because she is from God, and God is not bound by frivolous things such as time. So your entire life, she has lived somewhere, in the depths of your heart as a quiet secret you didn't know until the precise moment He revealed it to you. And that love, that beautiful, delicious, amazing, and frightening love, which makes you hurt in places deep in your soul you didn't know existed, does not just begin, but continues. It grows stronger and shouts out into the world - This! Is! My! Baby! Deo Gratias!

The fourth stage is like a culmination of all of that love that has been building up inside of you; from those long, long forty weeks of growing baby, to that long, (or if you're lucky, short), labor to bring him forth. The moment of delivery is like those big confetti poppers that burst forth with excitement and beauty. But the moment after, when all the confetti has fallen in a rainbow of beautiful color, and a hush has filled the room, with wonder and awe hanging all around you, *that,* mama, is what I am talking about.

My favorite fourth stage was with my fifth baby, though the labor with him was more difficult than I anticipated. That moment when his small, slippery body was pulled through the waters of the birthing tub, up into my arms, and then we were both nestled in the strength and gentleness of hubby's arms, that particular moment was most definitely my favorite. His labor had been a measure of intensity I had not anticipated, and so those moments after he finally came were so indelible. His little hand resting up by his forehead, his wrinkled brow, the face of God mirrored there in his. I fell in love with him a thousand more times in that moment. Then, love grew rapidly, multiplying by the nanosecond.

And that love? It never, ever ends.

Just a few months into his brand new life outside of the womb, I had a feeling of confusion over my place in this world and my lack of understanding: how God could think that I was capable of handling the care of yet another one of His precious gems, how my melancholy and anxiety had reared its head time and time again throughout my pregnancy, had gone away for a time, and came right back a month or so later. I wrote about the noise that bothered me, the way my newborn babe had spent his entire time inside of me confusing me with his stats, his movements, his position, only to continue his unpredictability through my entire labor with him. I was spent. I was overwhelmed. I had no idea how to go on, to continue to live, to continue to love. I knew I lacked so much.

Then, as I was writing all of this out, I had a sort of epiphany, a Holy Spirit prompting, where I suddenly remembered that I was meant to draw my strength from the Lord. He is, after all, the very One who gave me this number five, Who allowed all of the joys and all of the difficulties, and Who was right there with me through everything. He has been with me, shining the same love on me that He always has, reminding me of the love I, in turn, am to breathe into my vocation as a mother.

A mother's love is immeasurable. Yet we have a hard time really expressing this fact that there really is no limit. A baker mama might say she measures her love in the cups of flour for each cookie and birthday cake baked for her kids over the years. A painter mama might measure her love in brush strokes or cans of paint; portraits hanging in the studio, painstakingly worked and reworked for groceries or the electric bill. Writer mamas might say it's in the words. How many have I spilled out about my children over the years? How many have I penned and hidden in journals, tucked away in dusty boxes and end table drawers? But we all know...we know...there aren't enough cups of flour, paintings or lines of prose to really measure, to truly describe a mother's love.

I know there are so many mamas who are worried about having more children for the mere fact that they don't know how they'll love another baby as much as their first, or even their second, as if love has some sort of maximum capacity. But I'm here to tell you that love doesn't have a maximum capacity, and it does not divide between your children, or between people in general. It multiplies. The only factor that might change that equation is you and your willingness to love. If you have any idea of the measure of God's love (which, remember, is immeasurable), you understand. If we mirror the perfect, unconditional love of Him, it is completely unending.

While we are on the subject, let me convey to you a little piece of my understanding about God and His love, as it pertains to motherhood and babies. I am a broken human being. My past (and present) are littered with mistakes and sin, and only by the grace of God could my future not be. Yet if I rely on my feelings about this, I would be overwhelmed by the fact that I am not worthy of God's love, nor am I capable of loving Him. But here's the thing...real love, particularly God's love, which is the source of all love, is given freely despite our unworthiness. It covers all of our ugliness. It diminishes our inabilities as mere humans, and provides a vast expanse of capabilities, *especially* in the department of love. He loves us to such unfathomable depths, and yet, in order to give us even a taste of His tremendous love, He gives us tangible opportunities...like babies! Every single time I have had a baby, I have been given a deeper glimpse into the depths of love. I have been shown new ways to aspire to love. I have been given secrets buried deep below the difficulty of imperfect human love. I have been showered with immense opportunities to stretch myself beyond what I believe is my capacity to love. In other words, despite my being unworthy, in having each child, my understanding of the value of love has deepened, and my conviction and ability to love has abounded ever more.

And loving Him? Oh yes, we are most definitely capable of that! But I don't believe it's enough to just say,

"Yes, Lord, I love you." Especially because love is less of a feeling and more of an action, a choice we make to *do*. In the Gospel of John, the risen Jesus asks Peter several times if he really loves Him, and when Peter repeatedly says yes, He doesn't just finally say, "OK, Peter, I believe you," and leave it at that, does he? No. He gives Peter a job. He tells him what he must do to *show* his love. Even though Peter is sinful, *unworthy*, and had even denied Christ before His death, he knew in Jesus' forgiveness, Jesus was asking him to show his love for Him, even though Jesus knew it would not be perfect. And Peter became the rock on which the Church was built!

Our actions in life are not meant to *earn* God's love. We can't do that because He gives it freely. We aren't even worthy of it, but we somehow manage to possess His love anyway, certainly not of our own accord. Our actions are to *show* God that *we* love *Him*. He wants proof. He wants us to make conscious efforts to show Him that we do, indeed, love Him, and to teach others how to love Him, too. This is not for His benefit, but ours. God does not need our love. But *we* need our love of God.

One of the many things I absolutely love about our Catholic faith is that within its bounds, in every aspect, we are encouraged and taught how to show God our love. Our faith encourages us to not just focus on ourselves and how much He loves us, but more-so on how we can show Him, and the world, that we love Him. Everything our faith teaches serves to point us back to this. Sacrificing. Suffering. Offering it all up for the sake of others. Obedience to Holy Mother Church and Her teachings. Offering ourselves for the poor, the sick, the hungry. Offering our marriages and our children to Him. Honoring Mary, His Mother, the way He did.

There are so many facets of our faith that keep us from *just* resting in the knowledge that we are loved by God, which, if frequently done, will leave us with so much room to become stagnant. This doesn't mean that we shouldn't rest in that knowledge of His love, of course we should! But then we get back up. We *do*. We say to Him, "Yes, Lord, I love you too," by *showing* Him that love in our daily life. We are commanded to *know, love, and serve* the Lord. It's a basic teaching of the Faith, one we learn as small children in early Catechism. When we get to know the Lord, really know Him, we want to Love Him, and we love Him by serving Him.

The lives of the saints are amazing examples which show us how to love God. Especially in the lives of some of the women saints, we can see beautiful examples of how to love God specifically through our vocation of motherhood. The Blessed Mother, Mary, is the prime example of loving God in her motherhood. Look, also, at the lives of St. Monica and St. Rita: perfect examples of a mother's love to never give up, but to endure. St. Gianna is a wonderful example of a mother's sacrificial love. St. Zelie shows us how perfectly imperfect one can be in their vocation of motherhood and still become a saint! We only have to read her letters to understand how to live out our vocation of motherhood despite our failings, our feelings, and our imperfections. There are many more, too. The Catholic Faith has given us so many sources of comfort in these most beloved saints. Don't forget to ask for their intercession, and never underestimate it, either!

As mothers, loving God means loving these precious babes that He lent us. It means accepting and delving into this vocation deeper than just keeping them fed and dressed. Now, for all of you struggling, much as I have, with just doing the bare minimum at times, this idea isn't meant to upset you if you have circumstances which lead you to believe you are incapable of more than fulfilling those basic needs right now. God knows there have been times in my life, weeks, where I felt like all I was doing was keeping these precious babes alive. Sometimes, I really was, day after day, just going through those basic-need motions. But as I look back, I see that even in my darkest moments, there were many times I didn't just feed and dress them. I snuggled them, I listened to them, I read to them. I gave them whatever part of me I could offer. And above all, I prayed with them, and taught them to love God.

I think as mamas we are super hard on ourselves sometimes. But the thing about that is that God sees the reality, whereas our perception might often be somewhat skewed by our exhaustion or self-doubt. He sees our deliberate efforts, and also, when there really are practically none, in His infinite love and mercy, He forgives any failings when we take them to Him with true contrition. His love endures all things.

Pray, Always

Never give up prayer, and should you find dryness and difficulty, persevere in it for this very reason. God often desires to see what love your soul has, and love is not tried by ease and satisfaction.
~St. John of the Cross

Motherhood has a great many components, for which we are all somehow equipped. I look at my body, and marvel that it could carry and grow a human being within it. I think about the short hours of sleep I get and yet I am still able to plod along. I wonder at the fact that I have but two eyes and somehow still often know what goes on with my children behind me. (It's called intuition; the inner eyes of a mother!) And these hands, these arms; there are only two, and yet, somehow, they are enough for all of these babies of mine. But still, I think, surely, four or six would be more adequate! I used to think that God made a mistake, giving mothers but two arms. Then I realized that *it only takes two to clasp our hands in prayer!* Read that again and realize that, yes! Those tired, aching, possibly wrinkling hands we use to clean and cook, wipe noses and bottoms, hold babies and carry laundry, are even yet more powerful! Prayer is the most important tool we have in our bag on this journey. Even when we are doing our best and we still fall, prayer covers our shortcomings.

My main prayer as a mother is that God fills in the gaps where I fail. Because I do fail. A lot. There are times when I am lazy. There are times when I am selfish. Prideful. Angry. There are so many times when I fail to truly live out my vocation as a mother, and in doing so, I fail to show God my love for Him. But, oh, amazing grace! He gives us so much grace; and when we recognize our failings, we open ourselves up to the understanding that we can't do it without Him. He *wants* us to lean on Him. He knows it's too much for us to do on our own, and He never meant for us to. Every morning, I ask Him to fill me up so I can empty myself back out for my family. And He does. And in knowing that - knowing that even if there's no one else, there is a good, gracious, merciful Lord here with me through these long years - I have hope.

The following is a prayer I say every day. It is my personal prayer but I share it with you in hopes that you can take it and make it your own. Its effects have been powerful. In faith and hope, and with humility, I also pray that somewhere down the road, I will be able to look back and see even more of the ways in which God has used this meager prayer along the way to work His miracles in our life.

"Dear Lord, please fill me up so I can empty myself back out for my husband and my children, and in Your mercy, fill in the gaps where I fail. Help me to love them better than I do, and help me to love You above all things. I ask this through the generous and Immaculate Heart of Mary, my mother, and in Your Name. Amen."

The following are a couple of other ideas, which I have employed in my own daily prayer life; some at different points of the liturgical year and/or different seasons of my life, and encourage you to pick one, (or a few), that you would like to make a habit, if you aren't already doing them.

One is naptime prayer. We pray the rosary together as a family, usually in the evenings, but I will often pray an extra rosary at nap times. If you are like me, you usually have to nurse your babies to sleep. (Sometimes I lay down with toddlers until they fall asleep as well.) This could possibly mean up to three extra rosaries a day, if you are doing this every naptime. But even one extra would be so beneficial to the outlook of your daily life, not to mention the abundance of graces to fill your soul. If you're not used to praying the rosary so much, or at all, it will seem like a chore at first. But the more you pray, and the more devotion you have as you pray, it will become such a beautiful gift. I have also used this time to pray the Seven Sorrows of Mary, especially during Lent, and the month of September, which is dedicated to Our Lady of Sorrows.

Another prayer habit I have is that of praying novenas on a regular basis. They are a great source of consolation and faith, as we implore our favorite saints to intercede on our behalf. Usually, novenas begin nine days before the feast day of a saint. Some people choose to pray the nine days beginning *on* the feast day. Whichever you choose, you will find a novena to be a most efficacious way to petition God for your special needs, through the intercession of the saints.

Something else I try to do is practice the presence of God. This is like an on-going state of mental prayer for me, where I return to Him regularly as I go about my day. Sometimes it's in petition, sometimes in thanksgiving. Sometimes it's just to ask Him to be with me in certain moments of difficulty or loneliness. The more we return to Him, the closer we draw to Him, and the better equipped we are to live our vocation according to His will for our life. It doesn't mean we will not fail, and sometimes we get out of certain habits. But as long as we are trying, He will continue to offer us all the graces we need to come back to Him, to grow in Him, and to keep going.

If we think about it, our entire vocation as mothers can be the greatest prayer we could ever offer to the Lord. Not always perfect, faltering through our emotion, our exhaustion, our emptiness. But also fervent and hopeful, perpetual and deep. At times it will be of both thanksgiving and adoration, and others times, pleading and desperate. But each day, each moment offered to Him becomes a part of that utterance. And when we look back on these years, we will see the culmination of a beautiful prayer of love, sacrifice, humility, and thanksgiving; meagerly offered by our haggard souls and graciously accepted by our loving Lord.

Love and Order

The domestic virtues, exaggerated beyond their importance, can be the cause of deep emotional insecurity. Tidiness, cleanliness, routine, all are valuable and must be cultivated in the family; exaggerated, they can rob a home of all its warmth.
~Mary Reed Newland, We and Our Children

Because I usually have homebirths, preparing for labor is a bit different than if I were having a baby at a hospital. (I say 'usually' because my seventh baby was a hospital birth...more on that later.) By thirty-six weeks, when my midwives do a home visit, I am to have all my supplies and the room in which I plan to birth set up and ready for action. When my midwife comes, she checks everything over and makes sure that what I am responsible for is there, that I haven't forgotten anything. The main responsibility I have in this area is usually the birth kit, which is basically a bunch of medical supplies like latex gloves, gauze, measuring tape, etc. Along with that, I have to collect a few household things - bowls, bins, paper towels, towels, baby blankets, baby clothes. Everything is to be in some sort of order, the items used most within easy reach. If everything were not in order, it would be chaotic when it came time to give birth.

I also need to remember to keep the room itself in relative order, as well as my bathroom. This is generally a good idea for daily life anyway, of course, but especially if I am going to have a birth and utilize those rooms, they should be neat and orderly so as to prevent any hazards while I am in labor. I don't know about you, but I have about a week of 'nesting' at some point close to when I go into labor, so even if those rooms are spotless, I still somehow manage to find a way to clear them out, rearrange, dust, and vacuum for the millionth time. Order is important, and it is also part of our labor of love.

Speaking of our labor of love - it has taken me quite some time to understand how my vocation as a wife and mother, including the aspect of my staying at home to raise my children, should mirror not only the love of God, but the order of Him as well; for He *is* a God of order and it's within this order that we can find just another aspect of His love. The two, I believe, go hand in hand. It is one of the many things I love about our Catholic Faith, actually - how the orderly nature of our Faith exudes the beauty of God and His love for us. We are all united in one belief, one tradition, one system, one faith. There is no confusion. The succession of

Peter grounds us in one community where we find the *fullness* of God's truth.

Also, our obedience to the Church shows our love for God. I think about how my obedience to the teachings of the Church - that order, even when I *feel* defiant - is what has brought me through some very tough times. My love for the Lord leads to my obedience, and in turn, my faith is strengthened, as well as my relationship with Him. Sometimes in our faith walk, obedience is all we have. When our feelings have overwhelmed us, when we are confused, when life happenings make us question and doubt, when we want to just walk away from it all and join the chaos of the world, that choice to remain obedient, to continue our lives bound by the order of the Church, is what holds us in Christ, gives us grace, speaks to our spirit and fills our soul.

So how does this relate to the order of our homes? I am often asked about the keeping of a home with many children, as if having a clean home has to be at odds with having a lot of children. The truth is, it can be, but it doesn't have to be. Back in my young-mom years, I leaned on the excuse that my children needed me in order to all but shirk my duties as a housewife. Now, this isn't to mean that I never did anything to keep my home in order, but it seemed that if my babies needed me, (even if they really didn't *need* me), at a moment in which I was involved in a chore or tending to some other household business, I would have gladly dropped it all to sit with my baby for hours.

Mind you, I love order. I love being organized. But I found it overwhelming to figure out how to divide my attention. And because it is much easier to sit with a baby and do nothing, or play a game or read a book, I would *rather* do that. Later, when I had many young babies, it was all often so overwhelming that I just didn't even know where to start. But I realized that kind of chaos was taking a toll on my marriage, my home, my own sanity, and, in all honesty, even my children. I came to the understanding that things like doing laundry could be an opportunity for a prayer offering of love. Not love just for our family, but for the Lord. And, let's face it, sometimes we are so fed up with our kids that we don't *want* to do these things for them. This is where it is most important to remember that above all, we are indeed doing it for the Lord.

It's not just about the law in our Faith, and it's not just about the law of our home. It's about love. As a devout Catholic, I believe in the traditional idea of marriage and family; of being a helpmate to my husband, equal to him in dignity and worth, complementary to his nature, not better or worse. I also believe that it's my job to stay at home to nurture and raise our children, as well as to homeschool them, and to keep our home as well as I am able, so as to allow our children the feeling and assurance of safety, comfort and love. We sacrifice a lot as a family in order for this to remain our way of life. If you are reading this, perhaps you are in this same boat.

But it can be so overwhelming to keep up with the household, even just basic chores, when we have a lot of little bodies who are all too happy to help make a mess, and not so happy to help clean it up. There have been seasons of my life, even after my initial realization of the toll it was taking on my family, where our home, too often, was in disarray; where I just wasn't able to keep up with the tasks as well as I would have liked. And that's OK. It's OK for things to not be perfect. It's OK to not always have everything exactly how we'd like it to be. A spotlessly clean and well-organized house is certainly NOT the most important thing in the world.

I also believe there is a delicate balance between having a house full of God's love and a house with an ever-growing pile of dirty dishes or laundry, or toys strewn about. Having the privilege of staying at home with my children comes with some level of expectancy as to how I spend my time, but I am not so bound by a rigid idea of how things should be that I can't allot for *life*. My basement is a testament to that fact! And so are the dust bunnies often found gliding along the hardwood floors when vacuuming has been put off in favor of a moment's quiet or snuggling a sick child. There is much in my home I still need to get in order at times, even now. There are also many seasons when things are finally as such, but with the ever-changing dynamic, fall back out of order again with the next. It is a cycle, and one to which we must be pliable.

In other words, a God-honoring home doesn't consist *just* of order and tidiness, and it doesn't consist *just* of children and parents who love the Lord and mirror that in their daily life, (although the latter is certainly most important). It's a balance of both. There is room for the give and take. There is room for the extra-needy child who takes up all of her mother's attention while the laundry, still warm from the dryer, is left spread all over the bed, cooling and wrinkling as the minutes tick by. There is room for sick children and sleepless nights with teething babies, and perhaps even the need for mama to nap during the day, if you're so lucky to be able to. (I never am! Ha!) There's even room for bad days, when the heavy weight of our vocation has seeped into our world and zapped us of all motivation and joy. We can admit times like this happen, mama; it's OK! They just demand much more prayer, and that we be extra gentle with ourselves.

Most importantly, there is room for playfulness and simple attention; getting to know our kids and filling their hearts with our love. There's most definitely a delicate balance between all of that; and that balance is what brings congruity to a household and spares each family member the inevitability of feeling inadequate, undervalued, overworked, or burned out. I have definitely noticed I am more carefree and less stressed when our home is clean and organized. But I have also noticed how content and settled my kids are when I have given them my full attention even if it happens to be "chore time" when they ask for it. Kids' emotions and needs are not bound by schedules.

Having children who are more independent now has afforded me a little bit of a reprieve from the weight of all household responsibility. Chores for the children start around four years old here. At that time, it's really just if the child shows interest, and then they get a chore that is easy, like wiping down a cabinet face or sweeping under the table, or something they can help an older sibling do. But, even at two and a half/three years of age, my kids, wanting to be like their older siblings, have often asked for chores. It's hard, especially when they are that young, to give them stuff to do if you are like me and just want it done the way you like it to be done.

When my oldest was about four, she wanted to help me fold laundry. I was folding a load of towels and she excitedly asked if she could help. But I have this thing about towels. I like them folded a certain way. I like the way they look when their lines are straight and square, when they're all facing the same way in the pile. In any case, I let that sweet child help me fold those towels and when she asked me if she did a good job, I smiled wide and hugged her and said, 'you are amazing!' Now, were her piles neat and tidy, her towels square and straight? No. They weren't. But the joy with which she did that job, and the way she concentrated on it, the effort she put into it, made my mama heart so proud. She wanted to please me. She wanted to help. I didn't even refold them, either. I just put her messy piles into the linen closet along with mine and shut the door. After all, when we go to use a towel, it will get unfolded anyway. What's the big deal, right? In all honesty, it took a lot for me to think that way, to let that messy pile go in that closet, but I was learning a thing or two about letting go of control at the same time she was learning about order and tidiness. Thirteen years later, I'm still learning, and ironically, she is very, very tidy.

Each child has so much within him or her to please the Lord, even if their idea of a 'job well done' isn't the same as ours. If you are a mother of many little ones, give them chores! Relish the idea that you are raising little saints who value and love order as much as you do, and most importantly, as God does. However, along with order, you are teaching them love - to love you through their show of respect, to love each other in their servanthood, to love their family in their willingness to be part of a team to get things accomplished for the good of the entire home. I recently read a quote by St. Teresa of Calcutta - *"Wash the plate, not because it's dirty nor because you were told to, but because you love the person who will use it* next." What a wonderful thought, right?

Love and order definitely go hand in hand. If you're overwhelmed by your heavy load of responsibility in your home, take heart. Many children mean many hands, and many hands make light work. It's important for us to remember that, although we don't want to burden our children with so much work that they don't have down time or playtime or most importantly, prayer time, they do need to be taught the aspect of being part of a unit - a family who works together to keep order in the home. It not only teaches them to show their love for each other through their duties, but also, in a more practical sense, it helps them to grow up well-versed in the area of life responsibility.

It's OK to Stay Home

How can it be a large career to tell other people's children about the Rule of Three, and a small career to tell one's own children about the universe? How can it be broad to be the same thing to everyone, and narrow to be everything to someone? No; a woman's function is laborious, but because it is gigantic, not because it is minute.
~G.K. Chesterton

Late, on a warm Spring night in May of 2006, I called my nurse-midwife, desperate for her to come assist me in the delivery of my second-born. I had been laboring steadily for a few hours but had no idea what the rest of the labor would entail, as my first had gone so completely different than I had anticipated. She made her trek to our small condo and settled in for what would be a very long night. Throughout the night, she monitored me and the baby, fed me, encouraged me, supported me. Around 11:15 the next morning, cradled by my husband, I birthed our sweet first-born son in the comfort of my own bed in our second-floor condo. Though the hours had been long, I relished the entire process and realized I never again wanted to leave my home to birth another baby *unless it was absolutely necessary*.

Over the years, as I've chosen to continue to birth my babies at home, with a professional midwife overseeing the labor and delivery, I have been met with a lot of negativity from others. It's a hard sell in this day and age, when people believe modern medicine is the perfect answer to everything, to admit that staying home to birth a baby is your method of choice. Statistics show, however, that homebirths are just as safe as hospital births. But that's not the issue here. The issue is, everyone has an opinion, and as I stated in the beginning of my ramblings here, everyone thinks what you do with your family life is their business. This doesn't only relate to how many children, and location of birth, but also to one's choice to stay home with one's own children and raise them. No daycare. No nannies. No relatives or friends stepping in to fill in the gaps of time while we are out in the world. Just you and your sweet children, building a home life together. Most people don't understand.

When my oldest two were very young, I was told that we should put them in daycare so I can go back to work. It was a family member who said this to me, which, I think, hurt worse than a stranger saying so. As if my life's work, the care and devotion to my family and home, wasn't as important as my work out in the world would be. More money and the ability to take vacations was placed above being home with my children in the measure of value. It was a difficult concept to grasp, and an even harder one to battle.

When I found out I was pregnant with my first baby, I had been taking distance courses in Interior Design. My passion for creating warm and inviting spaces within a home, combined with my passion for helping others, was supposed to be my future. I wanted to start with interior decorating but not stop there. I love architecture, old homes, (especially antiquated farm houses), and wanted to pursue something combining all of those elements. I had a lot of dreams. But I set them aside so I could focus on raising my daughter and getting my life in order. I don't regret it one bit. I've been staying home and raising my family ever since. And guess what? I am often seen tapping into my creative side in order to design those same comforting, sacred spaces I've always dreamed of creating, and not for strangers or a paycheck, but for my beloved family and those we welcome into our home. It's not the life I had dreamed of. It is actually so much *more*.

It seems that in society today, we are told we shouldn't have to give up our other dreams and stay at home with our children. This is true. We don't *have* to. But maybe some of us *want* to. Maybe some of us know our calling is to focus one hundred percent of ourselves on our family and home life. That is OK! No, it's *more* than OK. It isn't a choice that is *less*. It isn't a decision that is uneducated, lazy, or born out of a sense of "settling" or "resigning" ourselves. It is a decision made out of prayer, humility, grace, and wisdom. I know mine is. Yours probably is, too! Society doesn't get to decide what we as Catholic women do with our family. God is the author of our life, and when we submit to Him and His will, the reward is so much greater than any sense of personal achievement, success, money, or accolades the world can give us.

Picture this: In Heaven, if by the grace of God we make it there, we will arrive with absolutely nothing. No diplomas, no bank account, not even a published book we penned or artwork we stroked across a canvas. We will approach our Lord on weak knees, bend low to His feet and offer Him our empty hands. In them, He will place the hearts and souls of all the little people He has entrusted to us in this valley. We examine those little souls, our vision magnified by His gentle grace. Will they be brimming or will they be deflated? Will we be able to say without a doubt that we tried to do everything within our power to fill them up as much as we are called to in our vocation, imperfections aside? Or will we have to answer so many questions on why we left them wanting, like thirsty sponges on the shoreline? If you know you are called to this life, and you answer that calling, forsaking personal achievements and the world's glaring eyes, you will know the answer to this.

In this modern day, there is also a bit of a push to 'have it all,' meaning to have both a career and a family. This in itself isn't a terrible idea, but can often be sought after in all the wrong ways. It's a fine line to walk; many cannot do it well. Moreover, there aren't many of us who are actually *called* to walk it, yet it seems that if that's *not* our call, or our choice, there is very little support or encouragement in that. I keep saying this in so many ways, but I'll say it again: when we are seeking God's will for our lives, humbly acknowledging and chasing whatever it is to which He is calling us, we have no need for the world to tell us it's OK. If I'm being honest, we truly don't even *need* each other for support. All we need is God. But! It is nice to have fellow women who speak up, give voice to, encourage and affirm us in this vocation, on this lonely path, acting as a means of God's tangible love, and oftentimes, His strength for the journey as well. This is especially true when there is not only a lack of support, but an actual effort to belittle us over our chosen path. A like-minded community is such a treasure, especially when we go against the grain of society, knowing in our hearts it is most definitely OK to stay home!

"*But who am I?*" You might find yourself asking this through the years. When the self you once knew is unrecognizable, when what you thought your life would look like is far from reality, when you wake up and aren't quite sure if you've lost yourself completely or just metamorphosed into a new you, you might hesitate. Get confused. Stall out. Start to doubt. *Who am I, really?* In these moments of doubt and confusion, it's crucial to return to the Lord. To sit at His precious, wounded feet, to pour out our hearts, and find ourselves in Him. He always has the answer; and it is always the same: We are His beloved daughters. His faithful servants in whom He is well pleased.

The Mystery of Labor

Love our lady. And she will obtain abundant grace
to help you conquer in your daily struggle.
~St. Josemaria Escriva

I don't know about you but I think that there is a profound sense of mystery surrounding labor. The method of gearing up for a birth, laboring, and then pushing that bright-eyed wonder out into the world is as awe-inspiring as it is difficult. Everything is new. Everything feels so electric and frazzled, sparkling like cool dew drops on blades of summer's emerald-green grass. You gear up, pack your bags, assemble your supplies, eat, drink, heave, sigh. You grab a hold of your husband's strong hand and together you coax the child into the world with shaking legs and furrowed brow; out of darkness, into light.

Suddenly, the pain, the exhaustion, none of that matters. What matters is you and that baby, and what she represents; along with the promises that are buried deep within her soul and the hope she imparts to the world. The number doesn't matter. This new life of number three, or six, or twelve is just as important, valuable, and worthwhile as baby number one. Even the general hardships of your life pale in comparison to the fact that you just collaborated with the God of the universe to grow and birth another human being. No matter how many children we have, this doesn't change.

The mystery in labor is that, though we are completely unprepared to take on the feat of bearing and raising children, it all disappears the second we see that sweet angelic face for the first time. Something once hidden is finally brought forth, and with it, so much understanding of the beauty of God's love and His creation. I think of all the things veiled in mystery: our Blessed Mother's Immaculate Conception, the Incarnation, most of the first thirty years of Christ's life, His original sacrifice, the Mass, His presence in all the tabernacles throughout the world. It makes me realize how blessed I am to have the understanding of this special and holy gift of motherhood. There is so much we don't know or understand along the way, and yet, when we are ready, (and willing!), God reveals to us all that we *need* to know.

Several years ago, a desire to be closer to our Blessed Mother grew within my heart. I wish I could say this desire was super driven, and that I started doing whatever I could to draw closer to her, but in reality, it wasn't, and I didn't. I grew up with a general love of Mary because she was Jesus' mother, and I obviously had knowledge of her blessed and holy place in the world. When I learned that my maternal grandfather had a special devotion to her, it awoke something within me, although I do not know exactly why. It was that information that led me to first seek out a deeper understanding of her, but it would be awhile until I developed any type of devotion to her. She was a mystery I felt inadequate to unveil.

Along the way, I have come across more information about some of the apparitions and miracles attributed to Mary. Such beautiful mystery, but also very humbling. I thought about how much Jesus must have loved His mother, and how much God favored her to even have asked her to be the mother of His Son. Because she is most definitely alive, and more-so than we are, it makes sense that He would use her to spread His message of love and salvation in the world; to allow Jesus to gift her motherhood to us as He hung, dying, on that cross. My path to a devotion was slow-plodding. But in realizing how much comfort and empathy I can find in her own vocation of motherhood, I was, and am, ever-seeking a deeper closeness to the mother of my Savior.

Nevertheless, it can be somewhat intimidating when you first think about her. After all, she is the mother of *God*. She was conceived without sin. How could I possibly live up to her standards? What do we possibly have in common? What could I glean from her that would not be significantly dwarfed by her sheer magnificence? But here is where God's perfection comes in! In Mary's life, she suffered and she had joy. OK, that sounds familiar, right? Motherhood can be summed up in just those two things - suffering and joy. Ah! A starting point! We learn of Mary's sufferings and her joys in the Bible and through our Tradition which is passed down through the ages. But we also have a specific and amazing tool at our disposal, one that draws from those events and helps us to focus on them: the Holy Rosary.

In June of 2016 my family and I were enrolled in the Confraternity of the Brown Scapular. That began our journey as a family to praying the rosary every single night, which has greatly deepened my love for Christ, and in turn, my love for Mary. As we recite and meditate on the mysteries of the rosary, I feel drawn closer to Christ in His suffering and in His glory, as well as to Mary in hers. The mysteries have helped me to relate to Mary on a more human level, diminishing my lack of confidence in her empathy. While our meditations should focus on Mary, and her son, Jesus, I think they can play an important role in drawing us into their hearts through the gift of empathy, and example. In our own lives, these mysteries can play an important role when we 'imitate what they contain': holiness, sacrifice, strength and joy. The Joyful Mysteries are some of my favorites, to which I parallel my own life, drawing me closer to our Lady. Allow me to remark on each Joyful mystery and tell you how I can relate to her in her joy as a mother, and perhaps you will find ways - general or specific - in which you can as well.

The first Joyful Mystery is the Annunciation. When the angel Gabriel approaches Mary and tells her of God's plan, asking her consent, she responds, *"Behold, I am the handmaid of the Lord; be it done unto me according to Thy word."* Her fiat - her complete abandonment to the will of God - is so inspiring, and if we think about it, we, too, abandon ourselves to the Lord in the same way, as we remain open to new life, each time we welcome a new baby into our family *no matter our circumstances*, each time we surrender our lives to God's will. I think back to that very first time I found out I was pregnant, and how it was somewhat of a surprise. Now, obviously, it wasn't a supernatural conception, and I was not asked to bear the Savior of the world. But, in understanding the joy that came to Mary through that unexpected circumstance, I understand the joy in my own. Mary said yes to God, even though she could have said no. As a young woman, I said yes to God in my first pregnancy, and as a married woman open to life, I continue to say yes, realizing the perfect joy that comes from each and every baby, even in the difficult times. I don't doubt that Mary was probably afraid at first, and wasn't sure how she would work out everything. She was betrothed to Joseph. What would he say? What would her parents say? She knew she could even face death over this pregnancy. But she trusted God and His promise. She trusted His perfect plan, even if she didn't know or understand it fully. Mary's ultimate 'yes' gives us the peace and strength to say yes to God no matter how difficult things may be, in whatever He asks of us.

Next is the Visitation. It is here in this visit to her cousin, Elizabeth, where we hear Mary's "Magnificat," and have a glimpse into her heart as the mother of the Savior of the world. Her humility is astounding, her love for the Lord, deep. She speaks of His greatness, and His mercy; how He keeps His promises, and lifts up the lowly. If we think about it, though we obviously are *not* chosen in the same way Mary was, we can still share in her praise of the Father, and also share in the fact that we, too, are chosen for something deeply intimate; something that is capable of expiation; something that is both humbling and rewarding. It is women who God chose to be the bearers of new life, who are able to share with Him in His creative power in a way no man can, and who He has allowed to grow and stretch outside of ourselves in so many ways through bearing and raising children, in order to bring glory to Him in that humility. And we can conform ourselves to Christ's sufferings, His cross, by gathering our own crosses throughout our vocation, (of which there are many!), and carrying them with love. As we humble ourselves to the glory of the Lord, we draw ever-closer to Mary's own heart. My favorite part of Mary's Magnificat is, *"the Mighty One has done great things for me, and Holy is His Name."* In our humility, the Lord does great things for us. Blessed be God!

The third Joyful Mystery is the Nativity. Here we are, back to labor! Mary was in an unknown land, far away from all family except for Joseph, when she gave birth to Jesus. She delivered Him in a lowly stable, surrounded by animals. We as Catholics believe that Mary gave birth without pain because she was not subject to the punishment due from original sin. But whether it was painful or not, it was still a tremendous feat to take on because of her circumstances. There she was, far from home, in a cave fit for animals, not a queen. She miraculously birthed her baby, and probably on the floor, in piercing cold, in the middle of the night. All she had was Joseph for guidance and support. I look at my own husband, Joseph, and think about how much of an amazing, strong, and loving support he is each time we go through the labor process, and I just know that if this man can be that for me, Mary's Joseph was most definitely that for her. She may have been afraid, just as we all are, but knowing she could trust him to take care of her must have been such a beautiful thing. In my own labors, I trusted that my husband's hand would be there each time I reached out to him, that he would support me as I shifted my weight, that he would catch our baby when I called to him that it was time. That bond between us speaks volumes, and can mirror the bond created between Mary and Joseph on one of the most holy and profoundly beautiful nights.

The fourth Joyful Mystery is the Presentation of our Lord. Mary and Joseph took Jesus to the temple in Jerusalem to be consecrated to God. Simeon told her of what was to come for Jesus, but Mary knew this act of obedience to the law, and to God, showed that she understood that Jesus was ultimately not hers, but belonged to the Creator of the world. Her trust and faith were perfect. So, too, do we understand that our children, each one of them, belong to God, and we are to offer them back to Him in recognition of this fact. This is especially comforting when we experience a loss of our tiny babies through miscarriage, or even the loss of a child born. Within the ache of my own devastating miscarriages, I find peace in knowing that those babies belong to God, and comfort in Mary's own acceptance of this for her divine Son. This fact of belonging reminds us, also, that the responsibility of our vocation is immense and our children are to be raised up for His glory. In this mystery we also find comfort in the fact that Mary knows the thoughts of our hearts. Recently, I was speaking with a friend about the fact that I used to find it so difficult to relate to Mary (and at times, in some things, still do). She reminded me that Mary knows our thoughts, and because of this, we can talk to her and ask her to be a mother to us, to help us in our own vocation as mothers, through our joys and sorrows, and especially in the mundane. Through her, God's grace is delivered in immeasurable ways, even if her circumstances weren't exactly the same as ours.

Finally, we have the Finding in the Temple. When Jesus was around twelve, he and his family were traveling home from Jerusalem when Mary realized that she had not seen her son for a long time. When she found that he wasn't with St. Joseph either, her mother-heart was sick with anxiety and she searched for three days among the people of Jerusalem, asking if they had seen Him. She finally found Him in the temple. What joy her heart must have felt to realize He was okay! I don't think I ever truly felt that same depth of joy, until I found my own son after searching for him for three hours one hot, summer day a number of years ago. He was a strong-willed six-year-old and had been upset with his sisters, so he decided he wanted to run away. He walked, barefoot in the blazing heat, three miles down the road to our friend's house and let himself into her home while no one was there. When I realized he was missing, I searched everywhere, calling out to him, but somehow knowing intuitively that he was not there. I called my husband, my mother, the police, and some good friends of ours. Within the hour, several people were here with us. I drove with one friend searching the roads, fields and streams near my home. A search team from the police department was already out, and a search and rescue helicopter was about to be sent up when the husband of the friend to whose house my son had run away called her and informed her that my son was in their home. I'll never forget the way my heart leapt into my throat the moment she told me he was found, and how I wept when I went to retrieve him. The joy in my heart overshadowed all the anxiety I had felt in those three agonizing hours. I remember praying repeated Hail Marys with my husband and I felt so close to Mary, feeling her empathy radiating down to me and back up to our Lord in prayer as she interceded for us.

Another little lesson to learn in that final mystery is this: EVEN the Mother of God lost track of her son! Think about that for a moment. Earlier, I stated that Mary is a little daunting to me because she was conceived without sin, and was chosen to be the mother to the Savior of the world. Her sheer eminence might sometimes make it seem hard to find empathy in her, to relate to her in this vocation. But, as I mentioned through these most joyful mysteries, and especially in this last one, there is much about Mary that allows us to draw close to her and look to her as our confidante. Even she lost her own son. What a humbling thought on which to meditate.

The Joyful Mysteries of the rosary are such amazing moments of Christ's life, carried in the depths of Mary's heart, which we can relate to and meditate on, and also draw from, in accordance with our own lives as mothers. Mary's own joy shows us that, despite any hardships we face, it is possible to find joy in our vocation. Through her Son, she was strengthened and uplifted, and now she resides as Queen of Heaven! We can also look at the Sorrowful Mysteries, and though we can't even imagine what it must have been like to be the mother of the Crucified Christ, having had to watch in anguish every heart-wrenching moment of the last hours of His life, we can draw from her sorrow and, in our own sorrows and sacrifices of motherhood, glean strength, understanding, and empathy from Our Lady.

Later, I will tell you a story of how my devotion has deepened over the last few years, and how she interceded for me in a very tangible way at a time when I was literally on death's doorstep.

The Longest Lent

Consider it pure joy, my brothers and sisters, whenever you face trials of many kinds, because you know that the testing of your faith produces perseverance.
~James 1: 2-3

The pain and sacrifice of the hours of labor are often wrought with feelings of doubt, inadequacy, fear, and sometimes even anger, especially at the transition phase. My first midwife was always aware of how close we were to birth when I hit that stage, as I audibly expressed how exhausted I was, and that I just couldn't do it any longer. During labor, we empty ourselves, sacrificing our entire bodies and everything we have within us with each contraction. In the process, we strip ourselves bare, and then we move through transition and suddenly, we have our prize - a beautiful, amazing gift that restores in us the strength we expended. A peace calms all those worries and self-doubt, and a new idea of love - *sacrificial* love - draws us ever closer to understanding Christ's own sacrifice. All of this is present, etched in the tiny face of our brand new babe!

But what of the next moment? And the days after that? The weeks and years we spend nursing, snuggling, bathing, teaching, and disciplining our sweet child, and then more children? We continue to strip ourselves bare, and sometimes, it is the Lord Who strips us bare in this vocation. The truth is, motherhood is difficult, and when facing something that is difficult, human nature often makes us feel a little afraid. We look down the long, dark corridor and reach into the space beside us, hoping there is a hand in which to clasp our own. When it's the corridor of labor, hopefully that hand is your husband, your midwife, your doula, someone who loves your heart and is trustworthy in the feat of guiding you through. It makes it easier. Somehow, you are not so afraid. When someone is with you, each step forward is much less scary.

In life, it is much the same. But sometimes, for whatever reason, there isn't a hand there to guide you. Maybe your friends don't understand your situation because they have chosen different paths or maybe they just aren't there yet. Or maybe they've already been there and have forgotten what it's like. Perhaps your siblings aren't there yet, either, or never will be. And maybe even your husband is often preoccupied with practical matters to understand your struggle. Sometimes you just have to have faith that, though you see no hand to hold, nothing tangible to which you can cling, you can walk through the corridor and come out on the other side unscathed. Because even though there is no human hand to hold, Christ is there holding not just your hand, but your whole life. Your feet, your movements, your meager steps, each is counted and upheld by the same hands and feet which were pierced through to save. To save *you.*

A few years ago, Judy, a dear friend of mine, told me that my current life-state sounded so much like Lent, she wondered what Lent actually looked like for me. If the truth be told, there are times even now that I am not so far off from the state that I was in back then. I try not to complain, but I think I had complained a lot in that year prior to our conversation. I was weak. Am weak. *But in my weakness, Christ's strength is made perfect.* I was at the point of throwing my hands up and shaking my fist at the sky. But one particular night, when I was about to do just that, I remembered Judy, who has been where I was, and who has been a steadfast fixture in my life for many years now, often encouraging me to just surrender. *Surrender.* So, I did. Palms up, in my kitchen, I surrendered.

The moment was heavy and broken. Shards of my life weighed me down. There I was, attempting to pull out a plastic cup which got lodged in the garbage disposal. This, after retreating from a battle with the hot water heater which was leaking all over the laundry room floor, soaking blankets and other random clothes awaiting wash. That, after spending the previous three days cleaning up puke and washing my hands a thousand times because my two boys had been sick, one even having to go to the hospital. And *all of that* after the previous two years of daily contention with extended family. I realize that these issues aren't huge compared to others'. I know this. But in that moment, that night, all of this made it feel like the weight of the world was on my shoulders; a cross I could no longer bear. And...even Christ needed help carrying His cross, didn't He?

So, there I was, trying to dislodge this cup which was the proverbial straw for me, and I felt like I might crumble. I was in the middle of this dark corridor of life, crying out into a vacuous space, when I heard a voice tell me to just surrender. I was being stripped bare. A lodged cup or a broken hot water heater, or even sick kids puking for three days, is *not* the end of the world. This I knew....

Strip me away, Lord. Strip me away.

Later that night, Judy lent me some really beautiful words. Words that soothed; like balm to my soul:

"Try to imagine that you are tending to Our Lord as He makes His way through the narrow streets toward Golgotha. Be Veronica...with every puke sheet you wash, every bottom you wipe, every drink of water you offer...tend to Jesus in His Passion. Imagine Our Blessed Mother and how her heart was aching to see His open flesh and dripping blood. Imagine how she, too, must have felt

that God, Her Father in Heaven was stripping her, like you, to bare bones that first Lent. Imagine how she must have felt that she could not bear one more moment. But, she did. And, so will you."

You know, every mama gets to that point where enough is enough is enough. It's one thing after another, and in this life of raising children and keeping a home, there are bound to be rough patches where things just keep rolling along, gathering momentum, pulling in anything and everything in their path: one big gigantic snowball looming and ready to roll over and crush you. Being stripped bare is no joke, mama, as I'm sure you well know. And if you are unwilling, it can be all the more painful and messy. But as I looked around my house: disheveled, filled with germs, laundry piling up, broken things to be fixed; and as I looked into the deepest darkest corners of my heart: my life, my personality, broken *me* to be fixed, I saw a mess, yes... but it was perhaps a beautiful mess to our Lord, something He could work with and make new. All this stripping down to bare bones was, and is, and will be teaching me something. Everything. I have to conform my sufferings to Christ's sufferings and continue down this dark corridor of labor, of life.

My friend had a few other words for me which gave me pause and made me think. As I meditated on them, they ushered in a new perspective: *"You are truly the Cyrenian;*

helping Jesus to carry His cross. It is good that you surrendered. He will provide the grace for you to persevere and because you are willing to accept that grace, you will make it through."

I am helping Christ carry His cross? Apparently, I am, and I have no doubt that He is, indeed, giving me grace. I have no doubt on that dark day when Jesus was crucified, Simon the Cyrenian was given multitudes of grace. That his selfless act of helping a broken Christ to literally carry the weight of the world up a mountain was more for his benefit than Jesus'. Simon himself was being stripped bare, even though he could not know this. What an amazing gift to a poor sinner to suddenly, without notice, be given the opportunity to carry Christ's cross!

But just like Simon, it is really hard to accept our crosses sometimes, I know. The world says to look for things that comfort us, to do what makes us happy, to just do whatever we want. It is a very lonely and difficult road to go against all of that, to accept, and, dare I say, rejoice in our sufferings. But the Lord was not beaten bloody and hung on a cross so we could have luxuries of this world and go through life carefree and at ease. His Passion was about something much deeper. In hanging on that cross, in allowing those soldiers to drive nails into His strong hands and feet, in humbling Himself, an innocent, in taking His last breaths for us, the sinners, He made it possible for us to one day make it to Heaven. This life we live is to prepare us to be worthy of such a gift, and our own sufferings are to strip us bare, yes, but just as a prerequisite to being elevated to what God has called us to be, to set us straight on the narrow path which leads to eternity in His kingdom.

The sufferings we experience, especially in this longest labor as mothers, be they marathon sickness, broken appliances, a miscarried baby, a difficult child, or rejection from family, are all meant to gift us with grace. To draw us to Christ. To bring us home. In our weakness of being stripped bare, we are made new and Christ's strength is seen. Oh, it's so easy to just do the bare-minimum, or to chase after that which makes our lives the easiest, or to even fall to pieces when bad times come our way. But we have to try not to run away from suffering. We have to stop living our lives trying to avoid every single uncomfortable thing. We must pick up that cross and allow ourselves the gift of suffering, the weakness and humility, the hardship. There is a point to it. When the gray skies clear and the heaviness has rolled away, there is light. A purpose. A hope. So, step forward into the darkness! Trudge on! Labor away! *You can do it!* He will give you grace and you *will* make it through. I promise.

Loaves of Bread

God's Providence is in all things; it's always present.
~St. Gianna Beretta Molla

At a typical hospital, there is no eating allowed during labor. My understanding of this is that, in case you end up with an emergency C-section, they don't want you throwing up and aspirating into your lungs. OK. Valid point. Except that aspiration with general anesthesia is not as common as you are made to believe. In addition, if you were randomly admitted as a non-pregnant person just after eating a big meal and you needed emergency surgery, they wouldn't put it off because you ate that big meal. The risks don't outweigh the benefits in that scenario, and in most pregnancies, they don't either. But I digress.

When I was transferred from the birth center to the hospital during my first labor, all ability to eat was put to a halt. For the next 14 hours or so, I could have nothing but ice. By the time I was in recovery from the C-section, I was famished. I wasn't even allowed to drink water, despite my excessive thirst, but was finally offered a popsicle more than

20 hours after I had eaten my last small snack. Then, for the next 24 hours or so, I was not allowed to eat anything solid because they wanted to make sure my bowels were working correctly first. The first meal I had was a Burger King burger and it was glorious! It was no matter that I didn't even like Burger King burgers. At all. But at that point, it might as well have been manna from Heaven!

So far, I have been enormously blessed to have had all but one of my subsequent babies at home with midwives who don't believe it's safe or effective to starve a pregnant woman in labor. Their philosophy allows for a pregnant mama in labor to have whatever she needs, including, and most especially, fuel for the journey. It makes sense, really. You spend your entire forty weeks of pregnancy readying your body for that tremendous exercise in which it will engage, eating every few hours, every single day, staying hydrated, getting enough protein. Just the act of growing a baby has been proven to use the same amount of energy as running a marathon. So what do you think happens when you go into labor? You are supposed to just all of a sudden stop refueling, stop nourishing and re-energizing your body? Now, I have heard that some hospitals are starting to change their policies which gives me great hope for mamas who choose to/have to birth there.

In any case, my long, long labors are not without some of my most favorite healthy snacks, hydrating juices, calming teas, and most especially good quality chocolate! I am partial to dark, fair-trade, preferably organic, chocolate with something yummy or exotic mixed in. I'm somewhat of a chocolate snob, so no Hershey's for me, thanks. To me, it's a terrible idea, going through labor and not being able to nibble a little something now and then. Protein to give me strength. A little honey or sugar to give me energy. It makes no sense to not be eating at this most crucial time.

Food is obviously essential to life, and in my family of siblings, food has a bit of a focus, especially for gatherings. What large family gathering is ever without food, right?! A lot of our focus on food is kind of a joke. We just really all love food, (I don't think to the point of gluttony?), and it's so obvious in our conversations, just how much. But, another reason food is kind of a family joke is actually rooted in something a little more serious. When we were growing up, the seven of us always had a sense of there not being enough food to go around. Now, my mom and my dad were pretty good about not letting on to the reality that they often had to stretch pieces of meat or cans of beans a little further than the average family, and much further than anyone these days could imagine. So, though it wasn't blatantly obvious, there was an unspoken sense of lack nonetheless.

I have a particular fond memory, though, which has also become somewhat of a joke in and of itself. There were times when my mom would get particularly creative with random ingredients. They would all get cooked and poured into this giant roasting pan which she would then place on the table, while we helped ourselves to what was there. Plates were used, but no fine china at the table for that bunch! We lovingly dubbed the pan 'the Ten Eyck trough.' My mom still demanded manners, for the most part, and we didn't actually eat from it like animals, of course. The name was given just because it truly was this giant, deep, trough - like roasting pan, placed in the middle of our table on the dining side of our small kitchen. Suffice it to say, there was definitely that feeling of a shortage oftentimes, no matter how elaborate and delicious mom could make the last few items of our pantry taste when thrown together. As adults, we often talk about the psychological component to how we each view food; how stressful it is to be at parties and, assessing the room-full of people and the contents of the food tables, start to get a little panicky thinking there just won't be enough.

Now, I must say, we never starved as children. There was always something. There were surely people in our world, and even in our own town, much worse off than we. And sometimes, there was more than enough food. (Feast or famine, I suppose) But I guess we just felt that, more times than not, there didn't *seem* to be. Having friends with two working parents and only one or two siblings, who always seemed to have much more food in their fridge and pantry than we did, and more exciting kinds at that, didn't help our perspective.

I think, also, about my parents. They must have felt pretty scared at the times when they found out they were expecting yet another baby. I know for a fact that they, too, did not have a lot of support within their families when it came to their family size. My mom once showed me a poem she wrote to their families to announce my existence. She expressed the fear that she didn't know what their parents would say, or how she and my dad would pay 'the fee' for my birth. She pleaded with her family to rejoice with them, as there was no other choice but to do so. Despite the hardships, joy was the goal. Babies are always blessings, even in the most meager and desperate circumstances.

There is an old saying: *"Every child born brings his loaf of bread with him."* I have seen several variations of this phrase, but they all mean the same thing – that we are not to worry about how to feed another new baby. When we are faithful, and put our trust in the Lord and His will for our lives, He takes care of us. Does this mean we don't ever have to suffer or sacrifice in some way? Absolutely not. We can all expect to suffer sometimes. But He is faithful, and when we follow His path, He truly does take care of us. His plan is so perfect, even though we often don't see it until after the fact. That is what faith is about. Trusting what we cannot see. When we can't see a way to make ends meet with a new baby just born, meals show up at our doors from friends and family, or gift cards and checks from strangers are found in the mail. In recounting moments from our growing up years, my mom once told me about the blessing of a fat wad of cash that randomly showed up in their mailbox from someone; no return address, no idea of who had sent it. That is a sovereign God right there in action, mama! I have so many more stories I could tell you of how God has provided us with necessities in the most amazing ways. His Providence is always evident.

Now, before you start thinking, 'But I don't want to rely on anyone else, it's not their problem!', or, 'We can't let other people take care of us,' let me tell you something. This is pride talking. This is fear. This is the belief that we are not all part of the body of Christ, and that here, now, on this earth, in this life, we aren't meant to care for each other. But we *are*! We are meant to build each other up. We are meant to bring others to Christ, to draw them into His perfect love. How else can we do that if we aren't helping each other and showing His love in action, right there in those moments of need? How else can we feed God's lambs, His sheep? Besides, if we are doing what God is asking us to do, then there is no such thing as relying on others. We rely on *God*. How He delivers is His business.

This type of pride is difficult to overcome. I've been there a thousand times, and I still go there sometimes. I remember one time, in my younger mama years, shortly after I had my fourth baby, I had a uterine infection. I had been up doing too much, not letting that gaping wound, that was the inside of my womb, heal. We had already had a string of meals coming into my home from loving, wonderful mamas from a group I was part of at the time. The meal train had just stopped, and then I was down for the count again, on strict orders from the doctor to stay in bed and rest. I remember when they brought the meals the first time, everyone was so amazed that I had been up and about when they'd come, and maybe even a few of them thought, 'Well, why am I bringing meals then if she can be up and cooking herself?' I got a little prideful about that notion. A little self-conscious. Perhaps I didn't *need* them after all. But then, there I was, back on my couch, unable to move, unable to do much more than nurse my baby and read to my other littles. Providentially, someone asked about starting meals again. I had to swallow such a huge lump of pride, I thought I might choke. But, back then, my handsome husband wasn't as much of a chef as he is now, and I definitely needed that extra help. So, I said yes. I said yes in my need, despite my pride, because I knew that, among other reasons, this was why the Lord put these ladies in my life at that time. I had no one else, as my family was too far away. They are who He sent to deliver His grace.

It wouldn't be too long after that my husband lost his job and the same group rallied again and brought us food, gift cards, care packages, and clothes for the kids. There have been other times as well, when we've found ourselves in situations where we needed help from others in various ways. Yet there have been many times the Lord has allowed us the blessing of being able to help others, as well. This is also a part of our life that is subject to the varying seasons. Sometimes, we are needy. Sometimes we are able to help others in need. The fact is, the Lord takes care of us. But He isn't down here walking the earth along with us, so He uses other people to do His work; ordinary people who are His eyes, His ears, His hands, His feet. Of course, we aren't meant to fall into a mentality of *purposeful* dependence on others, but when we do something that we know is His will, and it puts us in a place of need, we do depend on *Him* to see us through.

Yes, every baby does come with a loaf of bread under his or her arm. That saying, in whatever form, is meant to remind us that we have nothing to worry about. That if we take up our cross and follow Him, He will never forsake us. We have nothing to fear. For a more practical reminder, we can always look at Matthew 6:25-26: *"That is why I am telling you not to worry about your life and what you are to eat, nor about your body and what you are to wear. Surely life is more than food, and the body more than clothing! Look at the birds in the sky. They do not sow or reap or gather into barns; yet your Heavenly Father feeds them. Are you not worth much more than they are?"* Indeed, we are. You are. Your babies most definitely are.

As children, my siblings and I might not have felt like there was enough, but in reality, there was. Maybe not as much as most other families had. Definitely not as much as we always wanted. But we didn't starve. I don't even remember any specific instance in which I ever felt very hungry and couldn't be at least somewhat nourished. Thinking of history - times of war, and especially the time of the Great Depression, where food was scarce and people ate practically nothing, making soups out of water and scraps most of us would consider trash - I realize how lucky we are to live in these times instead. How grateful I am for that. This type of suffering serves to remind us that, though our 'quality of life' might not be what we perceive as the best, the Lord works through our sufferings and uses them for good. Always for good. Our suffering does have a purpose, all for His glory.

It's funny, but I'm pretty sure back in my childhood days, there was probably some sense of embarrassment about the Ten Eyck trough, especially if it was used when our friends were over. But years later, I have heard several of our childhood friends comment on how much they loved crowding in with us at that tiny table, and eating food my mom lovingly cooked for them as well, especially when it was served in the big trough. The other day I was at my mom's house and I noticed that beloved pan sitting on the counter. All I could think of was how small it seemed compared to my childhood memory of it. Make no mistake, it is quite a large pan, but as a child, it seemed so much larger. It made me smile seeing it there, still, after all these years, a fixture in their kitchen.

I look back on our life as a large family living on one income, far from perfection in every sense of the word, and I am grateful. I am grateful to have shared rooms, and even beds, with my sisters. I am grateful to have had to wear their hand-me-downs, to have had less food than the average family had at times., to have had more siblings than my friends had. Though our house was chaotic and messy, skeletons in our closets, secrets and baggage, there was so much love. So much. And my parents, God bless them, opened their door to anyone and everyone. My dad always said that they didn't have 'just seven' kids. There was a constant stream of random friends at our house almost all the time: friends who didn't have siblings, friends whose parents both worked, or were divorced, or weren't very nice, friends who always called my parents 'mom and dad', who ate our food and who fought with our siblings as if they were their own. And somehow, because of my parents' willingness to welcome in and love those friends, somehow, they too, came with bread under their arms. There was always room for one more. And truly, somehow, there was always enough.

Now, with babies of my own and living on one income, there have been times when I've had to learn to be creative with the last dregs of our pantry, the ability to grocery shop still days away. There were many times when I've had to humbly ask God to pull a 'five loaves' miracle right in my very own kitchen. In fact, I remember one particular night in 2009 when I was newly-pregnant with my fourth baby, He did just that. I was scrounging around for dinner and found one very small chicken breast left in the freezer, and not much else even in the pantry. Two old potatoes, a handful of baby carrots, a half of an onion. I had been flipping through my binder of recipes when I came across one for cream of chicken soup. Though I didn't end up making exactly that, using the recipe as a starting point, I did somehow end up making that tiny piece of chicken and those measly vegetables, plus some rough biscuits, into what seemed like a feast fit for a king. And all I can say is, the glory goes to God. The entire time I prayed, sizing up that impossibly-small chicken breast meant to feed the five of us, chopping up old potatoes and that half of an onion, and I thought of the parable of the five loaves and two fish. I just prayed and prayed that God would make it enough. And He did.

I think that by today's standards, we probably have been considered financially poor at times. But definitely not by the standards of the times of even my childhood, and if I'm being honest, I haven't *felt* poor. Of course, I get somewhat worrisome when bills come in higher than I expected, or when something breaks in the house or on a vehicle, or when not all of the services from a doctor's visit are covered by insurance, or when we are days away from being able to afford a grocery run and there is very little in the fridge or pantry. Oh, and that phenomenon of practically all the food disappearing from my fridge just a few days after a shop always rattles me. Where did it all go? My friend and I talk about this quite often. You get home from shopping, all the stuff gets put away, and you feel so joyous and blessed that your pantry and fridge are full, praise the Lord! But then, seemingly just two or three days later, it's no longer there. How does this happen?

Well, sometimes, we have to go without. Sometimes that thing that has broken doesn't get fixed right away and we have to compromise. Sometimes, those bills have to get paid late, or one dollar at a time. Sometimes what we perceive as a need is really, in the grand scheme of things, not. It is so difficult to live in a society of consumerism, and even when we feel like we are sacrificing and going without compared to our neighbors, the reality is that we could always give up more. It's hard to choose that. I know. It's so difficult to *want* to suffer, to *want* to be without. I think of saints like Francis of Assisi, the son of a wealthy merchant who gave up his inheritance, and essentially his family, to live a life of poverty, even wearing a garment made of horsehair as an act of self-imposed penance. His sacrifice was essential to His mission, which was to rebuild the Church. We can use his example of how he worked, to do that in our own quest to be part of building the Church, especially our own domestic Church as mothers. That doesn't mean we have to wear garments of horse hair! But it does give us an idea of the sacrifice and penance we should seek in our vocations, and as members of our faith communities.

Blessings abound in suffering and sacrifice. One year, our dishwasher broke and we could not afford to replace it. With many kids home all day, the dishes pile up quickly, so having a dishwasher is so convenient. When it broke, it was stressful at first. But really, it ended up being a blessing more than anything, in so many ways seen, and – I'm sure - unseen. My two oldest often had the task of washing and drying together, and the following year, when we finally did get a new one, they both said they missed the time they had to do the dishes as a team. Of course, there was sometimes fighting, as siblings are wont to do. But there was also camaraderie, and a shared sense of both begrudging duty and joyful accomplishment.

When I did the dishes, I discovered I really liked washing dishes by hand. I made a small wooden sign and put it in the garden window above the kitchen sink. On it I painted a quote by St. Teresa of Avila, *"God walks among the pots and pans."* I also painted some bubbles and small stacks of pots and pans, and when I realized I had painted exactly ten bubbles, I started using those bubbles as a guide to recite decades of the rosary or the Divine Mercy Chaplet while I spent my time at the sink, my hands deep in the soapy hot water. What was seen first as an inconvenience, yet another need we could not fill, took on a new vision as we realized the wisdom in the Lord's allowance for such a thing to happen. Years later, then with seven kids, we were back to hand-washing dishes, as yet another dishwasher had been on the fritz practically since we bought it. It was yet another good lesson in sacrifice, team-work, patience and responsibility for all of us, most especially the children.

Another thing to address along these lines is the fact that many of us have those fixtures in our lives of family or friends who have much to say in this area. Much of other people's comments of us having a large family is rooted in love, I'll give them that. But sometimes, it's also coming from a place of jealousy, fear, or even an idea of perfection about life that doesn't allow for more children who need to be fed, and where financially, it doesn't even make sense. They have such strong opinions about it that they are relentless in their attempts to control what we do. However, we need to understand something. There has to come a time when we realize that we are our own family, and that what other people think or say shouldn't matter more than what God says. We have to make our own choices. Those choices should never be made out of fear or coercion, but out of faith and love. When something makes sense to us or others, that doesn't necessarily mean God sees it the same way. Our mindset should be of wise stewardship, yes, but trumping that should be the question of what is God's will in this?

My husband was once offered to have a vasectomy paid for by someone. This was after baby number four. If you remember, earlier I mentioned that it was a very difficult time in our life financially, and we were also struggling in other ways, but that was unknown to the person. Their motivation for the offer is mostly unknown, except that some comments led us to believe that perhaps it was a sense of fear and a need to convey their idea of a perfect life which was already often thrust on us by them otherwise. We declined the invitation, feeling somewhat shocked and hurt, but mostly saddened. Looking back on that, I am so grateful that, even in our younger years, when our faith was still budding as a family, when things were so difficult for us, when it would have just been the easiest thing to do, God's grace was laid upon our hearts to say, *"no, thanks,"* and continue on the same path He had laid out for us the first time we rejected a worldly life. I am so thankful for my children who have been born since then, and even for the babies I lost. Our family looks exactly as God has willed, and not how others want it to. I am thankful, also, that our convictions in the teachings of Holy Mother Church were at least rooted deep enough to steer clear of even entertaining such an invitation to begin with.

Having many children, which allows our 'longest labors' to extend further and further with each new babe, is certainly not the easy path. It's kind of scary when you look at it on the surface. In those moments when it seems like one thing after another breaks down, bills start piling up, and we look at those many sweet faces with mouths needing to be fed, we might start to panic a little. But if we take that panic feeling and we replace it with trust and prayer, amazing things can happen. Having had the experience of some dire circumstances, having been on the brink of worry and frustration about how to make room, how to care for one more, I am blessed to be able to say with confidence that we have. We can. We will.

A Miracle Unfolding

The world's thy ship and not thy home.
~St. Therese of Lisieux

In April 2017, I found myself pregnant again after believing that I was incapable of having more babies. My youngest was almost three, (the biggest gap between pregnancies for me), and I had been very unwell for at least a year prior, with no answers from the medical community as to why I felt so terrible all the time or why my fertility had changed from what it had been. It was a time of excitement and fear as I wondered if I would be able to carry the baby to term, feeling as awful as I did. My husband and I had been going to the gym since that February, in an attempt to build up my strength and do whatever I could to feel better. Thanks be to God, I was able to continue attending the gym with slight adjustments to our workout, and felt well throughout most of my pregnancy.

However, that December, I gave birth to our ninth baby (seventh born) after a surprise induction due to high blood pressure and HELLP syndrome. Yes, this means I had to deliver at the hospital! I had gone to my thirty-six-week appointment that prior Friday, and my blood pressure was up after almost an entire pregnancy of being perfect. My midwife was cautiously optimistic that I was probably just under a lot of stress, (I was), and sent me home with instructions on how to try to get my blood pressure down over the weekend before I returned on Monday. Monday came and I went to my appointment with the idea that I was fine, that I'd be back home soon, get some stuff done and then get ready for a date with my husband, as it was our thirteenth wedding anniversary. But I wouldn't make it home that day, nor for another three. My blood pressure had climbed to the point of danger, and my midwife insisted we head to the hospital immediately. I was induced and put on magnesium. In the early hours of the following day, I was given Pitocin.

After that long labor, the doctor came in and talked to me about having a C-section. According to the monitors, the baby was in distress and it didn't look like I was doing so well myself. Despite spending most of my labor in a magnesium-induced fog, I'll never forget the memory of the peace I had in resigning myself to another C-section, nor the whirlwind that ensued just after the doctor urged me to consider it. You see, my homebirth midwife was with me there and asked the doctor if we could have a minute to digest the information and make a decision of consent. After the doctor made us understand the urgency of the matter, she left the room to call the anesthesiologist. Quickly, my midwife said a prayer and she and my sister, (who was there as my doula), left the room to give my husband and I a moment. I told my husband I was OK, though we both were crying over the idea of another C-section. Then something miraculous happened! Just as he was leaving the room to tell the doctor we were ready; he saw the baby's heart rate on the monitor jump up. At that same moment, I shouted that the baby was coming. Then I had a massive contraction that brought the baby inches from being born. Everyone rushed into the room, and in less than two minutes, she was born. Praise God!

Aside from being early, she was also very small at just five pounds one ounce; a whisper of a baby. I couldn't hold her without help, as I had so much magnesium coursing through my veins that I had lost all control of my limbs. The sweet tiny baby was checked out and found to be just fine. But unbeknownst to me, there was still more for me to overcome, and another miracle about to take place.

An hour or so after the birth, I sat up in bed, urging that something was terribly wrong, and within minutes, a crash team was called to my room as I became completely unresponsive. For over a half an hour, the team worked to figure out why I wasn't able to wake up. They finally concluded that maybe I had been overdosed on magnesium, and my organs had started shutting down. So they turned off my drip so they could have better chances of reviving me. Since that experience, and the aftermath of it, I have had some questions and reflections on life and death and my purpose here. But I have been very blessed to have some amazing people in my life who, at the most perfect moments, God uses to hand me a small morsel of an answer or encouragement along this path, including one of my beloved priests, who is always patient with my ramblings.

Recently, a dear friend related to me the idea that *we are all walking corpses. Memento mori,* which is Latin for, 'remember your death,' is something we are traditionally called to do as Catholics, but in modern times has not been something preached about or practiced among the majority. But truly, it is an essential practice if we want to understand how fragile and fleeting our life is, how each day is full of so many choices to sin or not, and that when we can contemplate our own mortality, our own death, it helps us to gain humility, as well as to choose rightly in our actions, thoughts and words. We are but dust and to dust we shall return.

Furthermore, we are to meditate on all four of the "last things": Death, Judgment, Heaven, and Hell. We travel this world, walking corpses, awaiting our death, and our eternity. We don't belong here; we are but wayfarers. Because Christ has overcome death, through Him, we have the option of Heaven, but we are not guaranteed Heaven, especially not *just because* we claim Him as Lord and Savior. Contemplating our death, understanding that we must die, imparts a generous gift to us if we would only reach out and take it: *humility*. With humility, we gain so much understanding, and our propensity toward sin is lessened, our walk with the Lord, closer. We are working out our salvation even in this task of contemplating death. It's a catalyst to a holy life, and to a saintly eternity.

So, you may ask, what does this have to do with my experience at my seventh birth? My friend lent the phrase '*we are all walking corpses*' to me in our exchange of thoughts on humility, but as I read her words, they struck me as something useful to my thoughts here on the earthly finality of death, as I all but succumbed to it an hour after giving birth. I was so blessed that in the beginning of my labor at the hospital, one of my priests visited me, gave me a blessing and heard my confession. I unfortunately did not get to receive our Lord in the Eucharist, but at least I was ready for death with a clean soul. I had no idea at the time how close to it I would come! But looking back on it now, I know everything each moment brought, most especially the visit from our priest and his hearing of my confession, was a blessing brought on by the perfect will of God. Also, death has become a consistent thought in my head, and I have to say that before now, I was just one within the masses who do not contemplate it much in this modern age. My experience, though scary and difficult, was a gift in this.

We are sometimes completely unaware of the fact that we are attempting to do as much as we can to control life. But if we stop and meditate on the fact that we truly are all just walking corpses, and take some moments to contemplate our death, we might be more inclined to let go of more, controlling what we actually can: *to not sin.* I couldn't control the outcome of my pregnancy and birth no matter how hard I tried. I couldn't keep from developing HELLP syndrome, and I certainly could not have stopped the events that transpired after the birth. When we are open to life, we are open to it - full stop. No conditions. We have to trust in God's will, live our life in abandonment to it, and rejoice in knowing He has everything in *His* control.

Remember when I wrote about God working all things for good? Aside from my shift in perspective about death, something else amazing came from my experience with my seventh baby. She happened to be born on the feast of Our Lady of Guadalupe. While I was unresponsive, I had an experience I can only describe as spiritual. I was conscious within my own mind, but in a dark place. It was just black and nothingness. I had thoughts running through my mind. I remember thinking that I was dying and that I was OK with it. But then I felt sort of warm and started thinking about my children and how I didn't want to leave them without a mother. It was a very strange sensation. The image of our Lady of Guadalupe appeared in the darkness, then many images of Our Lady, and some of the saints I am drawn to, and our Lord. Mind you, these were images like the ones I've seen on holy cards or as statues, they were not actually these beings visiting me. I was not spoken to or anything like that. It was like a movie reel of these images of beloved, holy individuals running through my mind. Our Lord's image appeared just once. Our lady was prominent in her various titles, and repeatedly presented. I started praying the Memorare over and over again, asking to be given back to my family. And then I heard someone calling my name. Before I knew it, my eyes were open and the nurses were pulling me up out of the darkness in my mind and present to the hospital room surroundings.

The most perfect will of God allowed His Mother, Mary, to be a mother to me in those moments, and comfort me with not only her presence, but in a way, the reminder of the communion of saints. I am of the belief that this was to assure me of God's will for my life, to remind me of Our Lady's intercession and prayers, and that of the saints. It speaks to God's glory, His providence and care, His mercy. I don't know exactly what it all means, and I remember meeting with one of our priests months later to try to figure it all out. But the more I spoke, the more I realized - and his focus on other aspects of our discussion confirmed - that I'm not meant to figure it out. We aren't meant to know God's every thought and plan for us. We just have to trust Him. We just have to go through life, seeking His adorable Face, and have faith that everything is within His will. His ways are not our ways, after all.

A year later, around the time of my daughter's first birthday, I was struggling emotionally. I randomly came across the words our lady of Guadalupe spoke to Juan Diego, and was immediately comforted by them: *"...nothing should frighten or grieve you. Let not your heart be disturbed. Am I not here, who is your mother?"* Our Lady has shown me in so many ways, through her intercession in my life, how much God loves me and is with me always, as well as she. She has been a great mother to me, and in turn, she has helped me to be a better mother to my own babes.

At this point in my writing this particular chapter, it has been almost three years since the humbling experience of birth and near-death. My baby's third birthday, and the feast of Our Lady of Guadalupe is coming up in less than two weeks. Last year at this time, my husband and I were in the process of doing a total consecration to Our Lady, and our first renewal will take place on this feast day. It has been a ridiculously crazy year, with a lot of things happening in the world. Much evil lurks and blares louder than ever before. Despite all of this, the Liturgical year is renewed. Advent has come upon us once again, and in this first week which holds a theme of Hope, I do feel incredibly hopeful. Over the past three years, I have drawn ever-closer to Mary. I have had yet another baby, and I have developed an unexpected and most beautiful addition to a long-desired plan of my heart, which I hope, through Mary's intercession, will be fulfilled in God's perfect timing.

Fear, Control, and Trust

I hereby command you: Be strong and courageous; do not be frightened or dismayed, for the Lord your God is with you wherever you go. ~Joshua 1:9

In the first chapter, I wrote that birth is somewhat terrifying to me. In reality, it's not so much the actual giving birth process, but the fact that everything that happens to my body in those hours of labor is completely out of my control. How long the labor lasts - not mine to control. How intense and frequent the waves of contractions are - not mine to control. How long it takes for baby to come - again, not mine to control. Will I throw up? Will my progression stall out? Will my baby be born with the cord wrapped around her neck, (one of them was!)? My body is doing its thing and all I can do is hang on for the ride. Why is this so terrifying to me? I have to admit that with each baby, it has become less terrifying and more awe-inspiring. There is still some of that fear, but, like I also wrote in that first chapter, it is more about what the next step is. Am I ready? Am I ready to raise another child, especially when much of what happens in life is just beyond my control?

When I was twenty-one, I went skydiving with some of my siblings. I was walking through a very strange and confusing part of my life, and I had this need to prove to myself that I wasn't afraid of anything. As the plane ascended to the jump point and the air grew thin and cold, I felt mostly excited and only slightly nervous. I inched my way toward the gaping hole of the plane in tandem with my jump partner who was literally holding my life in his arms, and I saw the world below us, the landscape stretching as far as the eye could see. With complete abandon I leapt from that plane, trusting that my partner would pull the ripcord when he was supposed to, and that we'd land with our feet safely planted on the ground. He had all control. I trusted a complete stranger with my life! Why was it so easy for me to do that? Why was it so easy to give a random stranger control of whether I lived or died, but in life, I often find it so difficult to relinquish my control to God?

When we think about the mundane, day-to-day grind of our life with our children, how much of it are we trying to control, and how much of it are we able to let go? It's a question I ask myself a lot, and sometimes when I realize the answer, I'm ashamed. Because in all honesty, there is always room for improvement. There is always some aspect of my life that I can give more of to God, but still hold tightly clutched to myself instead. And, if I'm really being honest, even if it's something I've given Him before, sometimes, I like to take it back. Sometimes, my wanderings through this often-desperate landscape find me stooping and grasping at all the aspects of my life I've already placed at His feet in trust and faith.

Where does this desperate need to control even come from? Most of the time, I think it is from fear. While fear has its place and a healthy dose of it can keep us out of trouble, it also can be a hindrance from us finding our way to the Lord. When we listen to our fears and we allow them to take control, we lose sight of the Lord and His will for our life. This type of fear is in total opposition to God's love and providence for our entire life. It's important to keep sight of the fact that He is King, that His will is in all things. He loves us with an everlasting, unconditional, and most beautiful love, the depths of which we cannot even fathom. He commands us, *"do not be afraid."* And when we release ourselves of our fear, when we give Him - through our own free will - our trustful surrender, He will take care of us. This is in the small things, and in the big. It's in our daily family life and all that entails, and it's in the big things that come along unexpectedly, especially as mothers. Funny how labor, the very thing that will bring our offspring into the world, is not only the beginning of our life as their mother, but the beginning of our loss of control as well.

In regards to relationships with our children, I want to share my heart here about something I only discovered when I was well into my motherhood journey. In fact, it is something I still can't seem to utilize on a habitual basis when it comes to parenting my children in love. Perhaps in discovering it here, you yourself can do better than I; and if you've already come to this realization and are utilizing it on your journey, I salute you, wise mama! I don't even remember the exact moment it dawned on me, but the lightning that struck me with it was powerful and convicting. It was also painful. It told me that much of my correcting of my children was actually unwarranted, and more profound was the discovery that it was rooted in my need to control. But, like the waves of contractions I cannot control during labor, there is much about our children that we just cannot control. I find that if I stop trying to control every single little detail of our life in our home, especially the varying (and sometimes trying) personalities of my children, the less flustered I am. Instead, I find peace that comes with an understanding of how children grow and develop, what affects them, how their brains work. That understanding can go hand-in-hand with letting go of control. They are synergistic in that when you do either one, you are naturally better at the other. This isn't to say rules and discipline are out the window. It just means that prudence and wisdom are both needed to discern the difference between being overbearing, and training our children in the right way to go.

Life *is* sometimes a scary thing to think about. Especially when it comes to our children. As parents, we have our children's best interest at heart. But sometimes, that best interest is overshadowed by our need to control, our need to have things look like we would have them look, our disinterest in allowing them to make mistakes or learn their own lessons because we are afraid to let them be hurt. But how many times has God let us make mistakes? How many times has He let us choose, even if it was the wrong thing, even if we got hurt? There is a lot to be learned about trust, about letting go of control and giving it to the Lord. It's hard sometimes, I know, but the more we do it, the more we find peace.

When we get caught up in making things look and be exactly how *we* want them, we often miss the most important aspect of the dynamic, and that is our relationship with our children. I think it's imperative to remember that how we feel about a certain situation is not more important than that relationship. Even if we're correcting without anger, if it's something that we're just trying to control that doesn't need to be controlled, it can harm our relationship. A few years ago, my oldest had just cleaned up in the kitchen when I noticed she had misplaced something of her dad's. Now, as I mentioned before, she is really good at being organized. But, I have to say that sometimes, I think she gets a little overzealous in her quest. This often leads to misplaced items whose whereabouts she can't remember, or throwing out something she didn't realize was important. In any case, I went into her room and asked her if she moved it. From behind the blanket she had hung to create a little fort around her bed, I heard her sigh and she hesitated to answer me, probably bracing herself for my frustration. I realized at that moment, though, that she didn't need me to correct her for the hundredth time on this. She was probably already feeling pretty lousy anyway having forgotten yet again what we've told her about moving our stuff. So, when she did finally answer me, I just said, "OK. Do you know where you put it?" and thanked her, and left the room.

To be honest, back then, I often got quite irritated at these happenings, simply because I didn't understand her and couldn't control what she did. Our sweet daughter will often forget stuff we say if some other part of her brain is struggling to focus on something, such as when she is cleaning. But my relationship with her, I have realized, should be at the forefront of my mind in those situations. My understanding of the way she thinks, her personality, and her needs, should all be part of the equation when I am dealing with her. I can't control her. I *can*, however, control myself. I have failed at this many times. That time, I succeeded, but it was difficult. This is an on-going process. But there has to be a balance of loving discipline and letting go.

When we talk about control in relation to family size, it's a much different sort of mental framework. It's funny sometimes to catch myself wondering about another pregnancy, how we will handle it, how we'll afford another baby, how my body, my health or even my mental stability will stand up. It's enough to make one pause at times, and like I have done, possibly go back through, picking up those things to try to fix or figure out ourselves, instead of trusting in the Lord. *What's around that next bend, God? I feel unsure, so let me just take this thing back from Your hands and sit down right here, and let me just make sure I'm comfortable and safe where things are familiar and I don't have to worry.*

Over the years, and more so in the past year, I have been approached by several friends and loved ones who, in their own journey of faith, have found themselves pausing in fear over the idea of being open to having another baby. The thoughts of these beautiful women vary in what drives their fear, though some are similar and overlap. Some have had losses and fear another, some have grown older and their youngest is in double digits or close to it, some have health issues, and some feel inept or incapable of adding to their already-full home. They've sought out my advice, my thoughts, asking me about my own fears, especially in regards to the time after my sickness and traumatic birth with my seventh baby. They ask questions such as, after my miscarriage, or after I hit 35, or when I found out I was pregnant with my eighth, *how did I feel*?

Let me just say one thing here. I am not a counselor nor a theologian. I am not an eloquent or profound speaker. I honestly have a hard time stringing words together in my brain to have a coherent generic conversation with even the closest of friends sometimes. Being given the opportunity to open my mouth to speak truth into the souls of these women who for some reason have sought out *me* to help them in their plight, is so humbling and also somewhat terrifying to me, even if only for a moment. I don't know much outside the scope of my own personal experience when it comes to having babies and trusting God in that, and in life in general. But feelings are easy for me to share. So, when they approach me, I take a deep breath, and I ask the Lord to help me be honest, while at the same time, foster His Love within their worried hearts. And I tell them the truth. And the truth is this: it is an on-going, life-long process to continually relinquish my feelings of fear and my control to the Lord. Life-long. Feelings are valid and have their place. Even fear. But fear is not meant to be the only deciding factor in life, so I simply ask for the grace to not let it be. Through prayer and consulting the teachings of the Church, I do what I find God is asking me to do, and I trust Him with the outcome. I trust in His infinite mercy, and His perfect abiding love. That's about it. That's my *modus operandi.*

After my seventh baby, I was reminded of something: We can make plans, and we can go about our busy, messy lives and try to maintain as much control over every single little detail as possible, but ultimately, we are not in control. Ultimately, there are bigger things in the works. Ultimately, our lives belong to Someone much higher than us, and we aren't meant to control everything. God is. The more control we give Him, the more we are opened up to understanding His love, His truth. Sometimes, it's those difficult happenings - or even a life-threatening one - that reminds us that focusing on our fear has no place in any part of our life. Most of the time, we don't get reminders of this in such a profound way as I did with the events of that birth, but those profound events are truly reminders that God is still on the throne, today, tomorrow, and always, and He will neither forsake us nor forget us; He truly has carved us into the palm of His hand. Sometimes saying yes to God takes us to places that are unimaginably scary. But it's in these places where true miracles occur.

One more thing: Being open to life also means being open to loss, another thing we can't control. When my eighth baby was just about to turn one, I had yet another miscarriage. It was at the end of a strange week filled with loss: A good friend had started what would be her own, long, drawn-out miscarriage. Another good friend's mom had died, and a few days after that, we had to put down our beloved dog. Then I lost the baby. A week later, grieving, I sat alone on a beach, gazing across the vast expanse of the ocean, with the starry night sky hanging low around me; and I let go of my grief. Because that baby - just like all my babies - belonged to God, after all, and I desperately needed the peace that comes with allowing that truth to heal my grief. This is a hard task, and grief is fickle, not usually allowing itself to be glossed over or pushed off. But I asked God for the grace to do just that, and He afforded it in abundance. Though I would never know my child's face, never feel their small fingers grab a hold of mine, never hear their laughter, I had to rest in the fact that God knew them even before He began to knit them in my womb, and He loved them much more than I ever could. This was enough. Loss is part of life, painful as it is. When we release our pain to the Lord and acknowledge His control in our life, a peace that surpasses all understanding seeps in, and with it, a deeper trust in His perfect will.

The Trap of Comparison

Be who God made you to be and you will set the world on fire. ~St. Catherine of Siena

My very first labor and delivery was the farthest thing from what I imagined it would be. I had chosen a birthing center over a hospital because it offered a nice, comfortable atmosphere which was much more conducive to a peaceful birthing process, with midwives whose model of care was more holistic, gentle, and personal than that of your average OB. But when my labor stalled out for so long, my midwife made the decision to transfer me to the hospital. As I explained in chapter two, everything went downhill from there. I ended up with an unnecessary C-section and a lot of birth trauma otherwise.

When my Bradley Natural Childbirth classmates and I got together for a reunion after we had all had our babies, I was exponentially disappointed in my story. Compared to mine, their birth experiences had been a cakewalk. In all honesty, I was jealous. It seemed like each of theirs had pretty much gone exactly how they hoped it would, and if not exactly, the deviations, at least, had not left them with a lot of trauma. But there I was, still recovering from the abuse, as well as a C-section, emotionally ravaged by my experience, mourning the loss of my ideal birth.

Comparing my experiences and my life situation to other's didn't end there, either. It's such a super easy thing to do, and I think it's also very human to do it. The problem with this, however, is that it opens the door to so many unpleasant - and often sinful - thoughts. When we have a large family, most of our life looks so much different than that of the average family's. We may have several friends or family members who seem to always be on vacation, always out to dinner, always doing something exciting. Their ability to do so might be because they have two kids compared to our five or ten, and/or can afford it. It's certainly a lot more affordable to do those things when you don't have all of those mouths to feed. The green monster, known as jealousy, sometimes creeps up behind us, and before we know it, we're bawling in front of the computer as we stroke our giant bellies impregnated with number eight, drooling over pictures of a friend's trip to Hawaii. Right? Well...I understand!

While I can't say I've ever done exactly that, the green monster has definitely snuck up on me more times than I can count while hearing of - or viewing evidence of - exciting adventures of someone else with "only" one or two children, or even none. While we have gone on some pretty fun adventures ourselves, the truth is, we just can't afford to take our entire family out often, or to many places, let alone on a consistent vacation. Having a fancy date night is even hard. But you know what? It's OK. It's good to remember that those vacation photos and $100 dinners don't fit too easily in our [nonexistent] pockets when on our way out of this life. It's also a good lesson in detachment.

I think about how easy it is to fall into this self-pity and comparison stuff, and I really believe that it is the devil's work to stay there. I would *like* to do a little boo-hoo and then move on. But, being a melancholic, my "comfort" zone is to stay for a while, and possibly even invest in some real estate there in that dark hole. So, it's a difficult fight against that temptation and those whisperings to stick around, and there is an exhaustive gathering of every ounce of borrowed strength as well as every prayer I can think of to climb back out and actually do that moving on. Sometimes, though, the damage is already done. The devil hates children. He hates the fact that humans can procreate. He hates all things beautiful. So, when we start to get jealous about other people's smaller families and their ability to do so many things, he pounces. He pulls up a nice comfortable chair and shows us some real estate magazines, showcasing something lovely that would look fabulous built right there in the darkness. But we must resist, mama! Resist that easy chair and that cozy dwelling on the brink of despair!

Now, my comparisons often feel somewhat justified, as I don't want fancy vacations or lots of extra money, or even a new wardrobe. I "just" want simple things: more room for my children to roam outside without difficult neighbors encroaching our life; to be able to pay an unexpected bill without wondering which other bill we'll have to pay late; to be able to help so many people we know who need it. My mental list seems, in my mind, justified. But therein lies the fault. My focus is on what *I* want to be able to do, which is mostly outside of our scope of ability. And yet, despite my understanding that we can do nothing without God, I still don't seem to consistently allow that to sink in, to influence my thoughts and feelings and behaviors in our circumstance.

How many times have you, dear mama, felt that you had your own list of "simple" wants, feeling justified in them, but have forgotten that God's plan is perfect, and where He had you in those moments was where He willed you to be? How many times have you, like me, forgotten that your suffering is important, needed, and beneficial to your life in Christ? In today's world, where a life of ease is consistently dangled in front of us, it is definitely a daunting task to keep sight of God's will for our life, and our desire to follow it, wherever it may lead. But, as children of God, as

Catholic women, we have the greatest source of everything we need to persist on our path, and to come back, if we ever stray a little: Grace. God's life in us. The supernatural source of ability when everything seems impossible.

Comparison carries with it the risk of causing us to fall through the cracks into a pit of depression and despair. It produces those fruits of general dissatisfaction and negativity in our lives that, if we're not careful, can grow large and overtake our daily life, causing that despair to darken every crevice of our vocation. After a particularly grueling trial with this myself, one day, a few years ago, I was picking up a basket of dirty clothes from our bedroom to take to the laundry. Gathering the stray items that had been tossed toward it and never made it in, I realized how suddenly joyful I felt. The Lord, Who is the source of joy, had given me a great gift. I realized how long it had been since I found joy in any of the mundane tasks I do in my daily life for my family. I realized how long it had been that I had been tarrying in that place of despair and depression, brought on by my consistent habit of comparison, and my inability to accept our current state. That mindset had caused me to lose confidence in my abilities, and to be unable to find joy in my vocational duties for a long time. So, the joy I finally felt after such an extent of time was a most welcome gift. Praise God for His provision in this!

We are who God made us to be, and our family life looks exactly like God wants it to because we have allowed His perfect will to guide us. When we are open to life, when we continue our labors through the years, His hand always ushers us along, gently and lovingly, caressing us into the next moment, the next day. We might miss out on a lot of worldly things, this is true. We might find ourselves in the humdrum of our day: noisy home, many hands grasping us and needing us and prodding us, another pile of laundry to fold, but that is where He wants us to be. The world is full of amazing adventures that often entice us out from underneath our laundry piles and out of the grasp of those many little hands. And that's OK. It's OK to be drawn to that. But try not to despair in it. Try not to wish you had that *instead.* Compare not your own circumstances to those of others, but thank the Lord that you are exactly where He wants you to be. Take the adventures that you are able to without neglecting your vocation, and be thankful you are able to have these respites from time to time *and* your full and busy life as a mama to many.

The truth is, sometimes the grass is greener on the other side, but this doesn't mean God wants us in that same green grass. Sometimes the verdant pastures He has for us are in different circumstances, a different direction, and always, always in His time. Take heart in knowing His perfect plan for your life is playing out right in the midst of your everyday.

Joy Amidst the Chaos

At dusk, weeping comes for the night; but at dawn, there is rejoicing. ~Psalm 30:6

Neither the flustered atmosphere of the hospital room just after I birthed my seventh baby, nor the fact that I could barely hold her due to the unrelenting numbness in my arms, could stand against the overwhelming joy I felt in my heart. The utter chaos that surrounded me in those first few moments may have been the backdrop for that beloved moment of meeting my precious babe, but I was mostly unaware. It was somewhat blurred, as in a photograph, where the only thing that matters was clear and in the foreground. I had my baby. And she had all of my focus.

But in daily life, chaos sometimes does make its way into our minds, doesn't it? I find that if I am not careful, I can slip suddenly and unsuspectingly beneath its murky, tumultuous waves within my small home, with my many children, and all of their busyness. Sometimes, because of this daily chaos, I find that discovering another baby growing in the secret of my womb does not always solicit that same generous portion of joy that birthing one does. I used to wonder if something was wrong with me in these moments. Maybe you wonder this, too, if you have ever stopped to think about being open to life, and how it does quite often equal a large family or having another baby after years of thinking there would be no more. But somehow, you find that you aren't enthusiastic about another positive test.

Dear mama, let me allay that worry: you are normal! An amazing mother of eleven, who loves each one of her children to a depth only other mothers can fathom, once assured me that it is not realistic to always be jumping for joy when the news of a new baby appears on the horizon. Since then, I have come to know many other amazing mothers who all love their children, but will admit to that idea as well. Yes, new life is always a blessing. Yes, God's plans are perfect. Yes, children bring so much love and happiness into our lives. But also, yes, we are normal to not always jump for joy upon learning of another baby's existence. We are not terrible mothers who do not love our children. We are just...human.

The reality is that motherhood is difficult. It's painful and messy. It's a process of letting go, stretching ourselves beyond what we ever knew we were capable of doing, dying to ourselves, breaking, growing. Doing it over again. Will we always have joy staring at that positive test? Maybe not. And that's OK. Have you ever known any mother to regret having any one of her children? Could you yourself ever look at any of those little souls in your keep, and wish they hadn't been born? Besides, there are plenty of other mothers ready to jump for joy *for* you, to encourage you, and to pray for you. Let them! Your joy will come, even if it's not until that wondrous moment of birth.

Joy is often hard to find in daily life, too, isn't it? Sometimes it likes to make a late entrance. But it always appears. It is there to be found in abundance. But it isn't always found at the surface. Sometimes we have to go digging for it. The important thing is that we do. In the most difficult seasons, when many hands are upon us, we're being pulled in so many different directions, our brains seem divided into a thousand tiny pieces and our hearts are broken over and over again, we have to dig, and keep digging, employing the use of an excavator if we must! And guess what? In this process of searching for joy, there are many gifts. Most beautiful of them is the close proximity in which we draw to our Heavenly Father through our perseverance and long-suffering. The further we go, and in abandoning ourselves to the care of Our Lady, and placing everything at the foot of the Cross, the more apt we are to uncover that joy.

I'll tell you a couple of practices that help me solicit that joy, and my hope is that if you adopt something similar, you will find it helps you, too. Every morning, after the kids and I are finished praying together, we state something we are thankful for. As usual, this practice was originally employed for what I thought would be the kids' sake, but I discovered that it has greatly benefited me as well. Being thankful for even the smallest things found in the everyday has a most profound effect upon the joy in a woman's heart. Hearing her children speak gratitude of their own lives penetrates even deeper.

Another very simple action is that of praying for peace of heart. Maintaining peace of heart is, at least for me, an on-going and often difficult process. So I continually pray for the grace I need to do that. There is also an abundance of spiritual books to read about peace of heart, several of which I have found incredibly helpful. One in particular is called, "*Searching for and Maintaining Peace: A Small Treatise on Peace of Heart*," written by Father Jacques Philippe. This booklet is short, but don't underestimate it! Anyone of us will find its powerful message both useful and encouraging, no matter where we are on our path to peace.

Peace of heart naturally paves the way for finding joy, even in the most difficult situations. It has a multitude of other benefits, not the least of which is the stronger ability for God's grace to work in us and through us. A peaceful heart which contemplates the will of God in all things and trusts His love and mercy is one that naturally lends itself to abiding joy.

The Lord is so generous in our journey, if we only turn to Him. I find myself contemplating more and more what I need to continue on, despite there being days when I have lost my peace and joy. There is so much that I don't need. But what I do need is simple: I need the sweet baby Jesus in all of His smallness and humanity to teach me about humility and service and joy; to show me what it means to be vulnerable and innocent and weak in order to grow in Him. I need the Christ-Crucified to show me how to carry my cross so well that He draws me close, and in the words of St. Teresa of Calcutta, "*so close to Him that He can kiss me.*" I need Him to give me strength, poured out from His precious wounds, so to continue on, no matter how many times I fall. And I need the Resurrected Christ to remind me of the glorious and *joyful* promise of Easter, to point me onward, always, to my eternity.

Humility in this Vocation

The way to Christ is first through humility, second through humility, and third through humility. If humility does not precede and accompany and follow every good work we do, if it is not before us to focus on, if it is not beside us to lean upon, if it is not behind us to fence us in, pride will wrench from our hand any good deed we do at the very moment we do it.
~St. Augustine

Giving birth is an event which requires a great deal of humility. We are put into a position of reliance on other people, and we are extremely vulnerable. We strip ourselves of any pretense of a comfort zone in a number of ways. Aside from the physical aspect of having to show more of our body to someone other than our spouse in such an intimate and vulnerable way, we are coaxed into letting go of at least some of the boundaries we may have of our emotional parts as well. If you, like me, are somewhat guarded in those places deep down within your heart, you might find it a little unnerving to have witnesses to moments during your labor where your emotions are sporadic, chaotic, and raw. The first time I had to squelch my reluctance and become vulnerable in order to have help in labor was very difficult for me, both physically and emotionally. It still is every time I give birth, but it has gotten easier. There is somewhat of a natural process to this anyway, hormones and what not; am I right?! You reach a point in labor when you mostly don't care. Regardless, it's humbling to be in such a state of vulnerability and discomfort.

If we look deeper, we also see that we open ourselves up to an even greater act of humility through labor, and in our vocation as a whole, in the transforming of our very souls into servants of God. Through our openness to life, through our growing of a tiny baby within our very own womb, through that labor process to birth these babes into the world, and in raising them for His glory, we are *serving* Him. That transformative process reminds us of Mary, and how her saying yes to God in Christ's conception and birth placed her on a trajectory to greatness. Remember that that greatness began in her home, with a baby in her womb and the everyday tasks of her vocation, and was only realized in its full glory in Heaven.

I recently discovered a wonderful poem that really spoke to me of this idea of transformation and humility. My friend, Ann, had posted an Advent Poem on social media, and within it, I found a beautiful meditation not only for Advent, but more so, for my life as a mother. The following are the words, which are attributed to St. John of the Cross, as translated by Daniel Ladinsky:

If you want, the Virgin will come walking down the road,
pregnant with the Holy and say,
"I need shelter for the night.
Please take me inside your heart, my time is so close."
Then, under the roof of your soul,
you will witness the sublime intimacy,
the divine, the Christ, taking birth forever,
as she grasps your hand for help,
for each of us is the midwife of God, each of us.
Yes, there, under the dome of your being,
does creation come into existence eternally,
through your womb, dear pilgrim,
the sacred womb of your soul,
as God grasps our arms for help:
for each of us is His beloved servant never far.
If you want, the virgin will come walking down the street,
pregnant with Light, and sing!

Read it again. See how it's an invitation: *Allow our lady to be sheltered within our hearts, and she will give us a great gift. For in her womb is the Light Who burns eternal. In her womb is Joy Who sings to us in our miseries. In her womb is Love Who bends low in His own humility and gathers us to Him, hiding us within His sacred wounds. In her womb is our Savior, Who sheds His blood for us, beckoning for us to come, sit at His precious wounded feet, and be made new.*

All this, so that we might become the vessel through which our dear Lord showers His light, His joy, and His love to those in our keep; that we might create a sacred space within our homes where every member, in our humility, desires *only* to be servants of God, and through that humble servanthood, glorify Him. Think of that Light with Whom Mary is pregnant, His own humble beginning as a poor babe born in a lowly stable, that sacred space He created just by being there. Through His beginning, we are called to our own humble existence, so that by His sacrificial life, particularly that of His ending, we can share in His glorious Kingdom for all eternity.

But you may ask, what about now? What of the world? What of the challenge to give up our vocation within our homes for all that glitters *out there*? Or, even more simply, maybe you've stopped for a moment in the midst of life's daily grind, and thought, 'gosh, I feel really small and insignificant, maybe even a bit broken and fragile?' In the day to day chores, responsibilities, neediness, and weight, it suddenly looms larger than you ever realized, that you are but a tiny pebble along the shoreline of life's vast and expansive ocean. They can be quite unsettling, these moments, and if we're not careful, they have the potential to lead us to the type of melancholy that grows from pride, especially if we're naturally prone to melancholy in general.

But! When we seek to live out our vocation in a way that is pleasing to the Lord, to be that servant *in our homes*, embracing our littleness and triumphing against the temptations of the world, these moments also have the potential to truly offer us that special gift of humility, which is much-needed, and is often-times our saving grace. That smallness we feel, that fragility, has the power to transform our hearts and minds into a vessel through which the Lord works to instill in us - and by our example, in our children - the pure heart of a humble servant. It opens us up to the depths of our vocation that we might not reach otherwise. Then, also, the cacophony of the world becomes a whisper, and the glitter fades. What is left in their place is emptiness, the echo of which dies against the fullness of our life at home with our children. We see the facade for what it was: a distraction to hide the ugliness hidden in the siren's call of the world. Then, through the veil, we hear the joyful, holy song of sacrificial motherhood, which Mary herself is singing.

St. Padre Pio once said, *"You must always humble yourself lovingly before God and before men, because God speaks only to those who are truly humble and He enriches them with His gifts."* and, *"As gifts increase in you, let your humility grow, for you must consider that everything is given to you on loan."*

Everything is given to us on loan. That includes our children, who are precious gifts from Almighty God. They are created in His image and likeness, and for His own glory. Our role as parents to lovingly discipline our children is an especially great opportunity to acknowledge that fact. Though, often we find ourselves staring into the face of a defiant, worldly little being who has given into rash, selfish behavior, we have to look for the beautiful face of our Lord beyond - the *Imago Dei*; humble ourselves past our feelings of agitation or anger, and respond to our babes as our Lord responds to us when we have chosen the wrong path. This comes with self-discipline, and, equally important, a level of humility. We might feel the weight of our failings, our lack. Some of us might also recognize that the examples set for us growing up might not have been the best. But in humbling ourselves to act on those realizations and admissions, God will generously shower us with grace. And through it, we will have the ability to fulfill all the duties of our vocation, especially that of *lovingly* disciplining our children.

This humble submission is especially important when we get to the pre-teen and teenage years. These years are not for the faint of heart! We find in them the need to draw ever closer to our Lord, and also to His mother, Mary. Sometimes, even the children with the most generous and sacrificial hearts can have moments when their behavior or words cut like a knife. You may know those moments, the ones that break your heart and bring you to your knees in a way the "terrible twos" or "threenager" years never did. I am slowly learning all of the varying algorithms of the hearts and minds of teens and preteens as experienced from a mother's perspective, and I beg the Lord daily for both humility and grace when it comes to responding to those which are more than a little vexing.

Humility in this vocation of motherhood is imperative. We have to recognize that we can only do what God wills us to do, and that everything we have and are, is from Him. When we unpack what that truly means, we will never give up, despite many instances where we are brought to the brink and tempted to do so. This goes for our marriage, and it goes for our child-rearing. It is important to continuously return to the Lord and ask for humility, because with it comes courage, wisdom and strength, which are also quite necessary in our journey, (especially when we're outnumbered by our offspring!)

I have been striving to do a couple of things daily to gain what I need for my journey, which I encourage you to consider adding to your own routine: One, with every recitation of my rosary, I consecrate my children to Mary, and in doing so, I admit that she can be the mother I often fail to be. I ask her to hide them within her mantle and keep them close to her, believing that no matter how far they may stray, in her love and guidance she will lead our children home to Jesus. Another is to ask for God's mercy on each of my children. Daily. I need to be more habitual about these two acts. I also pray the Litany of Humility every day. Humility is an on-going lesson, and one in which we might backtrack if we're not careful. The prayers of a mother are so efficacious and we should never fail to believe that fact. God will shower our children with His mercy through our meager prayers. These acts of humility, of acknowledging that the precious souls of my children actually belong to God, and that I can't be a perfect mother here on earth, create in me a vulnerability. But with it comes a renewed sense of faith and trust, one through which I can truly call to Jesus in confidence: *Oh Jesus, meek and humble of heart, hear me...*

Here is something else to remember: Our lady was not an earthly queen. She was a humble servant. She knew hard work, sacrifice, and pain. In her humility, she referred to herself as a "handmaid of the Lord". She thoroughly lived out the words of St. John, *"He must increase, but I must decrease."* Yet she was chosen for a greater purpose - The Great Purpose - and she said yes. For us, the words of both her *Fiat* and of her *Magnificat* echo through the ages, resounding harmoniously in our hearts and within the walls of our home. They are words of true humility. In our vocation, we can also say yes, and with the effects of our concession we can say, *"The Almighty has done great things for me, and Holy is His Name."*

The Churching of Women

The most beautiful act of faith is the one made
in darkness, in sacrifice,
and with extreme effort. ~St. Padre Pio

The sprinkling of holy water. A candle lit. Holding onto the priest's embroidered stole. A long, slow procession down the darkened aisle of a 100-year-old church, toward the Beloved. Kneeling at the altar rail. Whispers in Latin. More holy water. An emotional, "Amen." My tiny baby, placed on Mary's altar to consecrate her to the Blessed Mother.

These are snippets of memories I have from my very first experience of the ceremony known as the Churching of Women. If you are not familiar with this, it is a ceremony wherein the mother, after recovering from childbirth, makes her first visit to the church for a special blessing from the priest. I love how this, in ways, mirrors Mary's trip to the temple in the Jewish tradition, yet is also a contrast in that it is renewed in the Church as a traditional ceremony for thanksgiving and blessing, rather than a ritual of purification. It is beautiful, and I really have no words eloquent or adequate enough to describe it in a way that conveys how sacred and awe-inspiring it truly is. I highly recommend researching it for yourself and discovering this invaluable gift. Furthermore, I encourage you to ask your priest to bestow it upon you with your next child.

When I experienced Churching for the first time, I was very sick. It was just under three weeks after my seventh baby's birth. It was such an effort to even be mentally present, let alone make that walk down the aisle. We had our baby baptized moments before, as well. The traditional rite of baptism is a little lengthy, so naturally I was exhausted, and everything in me ached. But within my heart, I had joy. I had peace. I was filled with so much gratitude. When we completed the ceremony, I felt renewed. I prayed in true thanksgiving for the grace to have made it through labor and delivery, and the event afterward, and for my baby, who also survived and was miraculously healthy, despite her early birth and small size. I prayed in faith that God would yet have more graces in store for us.

It has taken me a little while to look back and discover that I missed out on a great opportunity at that ceremony to pray, not only in thanksgiving for the things I mentioned above, but also for the fact that that birth broke me. It really did. It shattered me into a million pieces and left me there for a while, wondering if I would ever feel whole again. I am constantly lacking when it comes to viewing suffering through a lens of thanksgiving, though I know we should. Constantly. But now, these years later, I am in awe of the breaking. I am in awe of the renewing. I'm in awe of how far God has brought me since then. I don't always feel like 'myself.' In fact, I often feel very weak, especially when I realize that I haven't felt like myself *since* that event. And therein lies the reason to be thankful. *In my weakness, His strength is made perfect, remember?*

As I grew to realize that my weakness, my restlessness, my not feeling myself, were actually good things, I have also been repeatedly reminded of the words of St. Augustine of Hippo, *"You have made us for Yourself, O Lord, and our heart is restless until it rests in You."* Outside of God, we are nothing. The world offers us nothing to make us whole, to quiet our inner agitations and confusion, to give us strength along our path. Only God can do that. Though we face many trials which seem to stir up these feelings within us, when we rest in the Lord and have faith in His numerous provisions which He so lovingly and generously offers, we arrive at an understanding of who we are in His perfect creation, and we also develop abiding trust in Him. Though we may shrink and quaver in the face of our trials, we still know He is with us.

The landscape of our path to the Lord will look different at each stage of our life. Just as that walk down the aisle toward Christ to receive that postpartum blessing was for me, our walk in life is often going to be difficult and exhausting. Each thorn that pricks us, each rock we stumble upon, each cause for suffering, is meant to change us, to make us better, to draw us ever-closer to Him. Sometimes, the suffering is small and we hardly notice the changes within us. Sometimes the suffering is big, but maybe even then we aren't sure of what has come of it. For me, with that birth and subsequent event, the ability to view death in a different light was just the beginning. The weakness I felt, and still often feel, is a gentle reminder that I am not ever meant to rely on my own faculties. We are meant to ask Christ for everything we need, trust in Him to provide it, and pray in thanksgiving, (even ahead of time), for His faith and provision. Pray in faith, even in the darkness, and know He will respond. Then, we are more equipped to see our path illuminated by the light of His love, and see Him there at the end of the darkness, awaiting the moment He will make new, these haggard, desperate souls of ours.

Because the prayers for the Churching of Women are in Latin, I never understood the words, as I was too enthralled with the ceremony to follow along in a book. I have looked up the ritual since, and within the rich text of the final prayer, I found an immense treasure trove of abundant blessing and great cause for hope in my journey, and my final destination. That God has "*turned into joy the pains of the faithful in childbirth*" speaks of His mercy. It speaks of His love in creating a path which brings a woman full circle, from the joy of new life within her to the joy of holding it in her arms, from raising that little soul for the Lord, to eternal life with them, in His arms. This prayer also invokes Mary, that by her "*merits and intercession,*" we and our children may arrive *"at the joys of everlasting happiness."*

The joys of everlasting happiness. How sweet this sounds! How blessed we are to have such a prayer said over us by a good and holy priest! How honored we mothers should feel in knowing that this ceremony was instituted by the Church for us alone! As Catholics, we have access to a deep well of beautiful treasures within our Faith. There is so much about our Tradition and our ceremony that showers us with the love of God, fills us with so many graces, and encourages us to continue to walk in faith, this difficult, broken, and sometimes lonely, path to Heaven, despite how weak we may feel at any stage along the way.

The Interior Life

By habitually thinking of the presence of God,
we succeed in praying twenty-four hours a day.
~St. Paul of the Cross

My labor with my eighth baby was much shorter and much easier than any other labor. On the one hand, contractions began late at night, which is never fun. It is difficult to go through an entire day of regular busy life, only to begin labor at the end, and possibly go through an entire night in the throes of it. But the Lord was merciful to me. After a friend came and picked up all but one of my children, we settled into a rhythm of walking, praying, hydrating, eating, and resting. I shifted and stirred in specific ways to encourage proper positioning of the baby, and before I knew it, my midwife and her assistant were at my home. Then, I was climbing into the birth tub to begin a new rhythm of praying, sighing, and waiting. My baby came shortly thereafter.

I truly believe that my labor was so calm and short and easy - a much different experience than I'm used to -

because my soul was open to the Lord's promptings; enough so, that when He placed upon it a request to use my time in labor to pray for others' intentions, I happily complied. Weeks before, I had sent out an email and a social media post requesting intentions for which to pray, and was so humbled to receive quite a number of them. Little did I know that in this request, He had hidden a gift for me of having a short and easy labor. I spent most of it in prayer for other people. At first, I read the paper upon which I recorded the intentions. Then, as labor intensified and I found it hard to concentrate on holding and reading a piece of paper, I tried to memorize them and kept them in my mind as I circled through them one by one, again and again. I remember at some points picturing some of the people who had entrusted to me their most special intentions, and I felt so much joy, confident that the Lord would answer them in His perfect way and time.

Having gone through seven labors before this, I have to say that it is no easy feat to concentrate on something or someone else while in labor. It takes a great deal of focus, interior quiet and most of all, a sincere reliance upon the Lord. If you think about it, this also applies to life in general, and our focus on what is most important: our vocation. Our ability to do so *well* lies mainly in our interior life. Admittedly, as a busy mother, over the years I found it very difficult to give a lot of attention to my interior life, especially when my understanding of the Faith was so lacking and I had a lot of little children gobbling up my attention. However, in my journey, especially that of the last few years, as I have grown closer to our Lord, as I have developed a more solid personal prayer habit, I have felt my soul more able to feel His presence and hear His promptings. In reality, it is precisely because we are so busy and our children so desperately need much of our attention, that we should be working on our interior life consistently. St. Francis de Sales said that we all need thirty minutes of prayer a day, but if we're busy, we need an hour. Think about that!

As mothers in charge of even just one soul, we are called to a specific work, whose greatness can only be achieved through an interior life grounded in Christ. Everything we do must be rooted in the heart of God, and our relationship with Him, or it will not succeed. All ends must justify the means. All ends should be that which brings God glory, and therefore, all means should be driven by a genuine and sincere, solid and deep interior life. When our work, our vocation, is built upon such a spiritual life, God will bless it.

So how do we get there, if we aren't blessed to be there already? I, myself, am not exactly where I want to be, or know I should be, when it comes to the state of my interior life. I'm admittedly still in what are probably the infant stages of this particular aspect of my journey. So, I mostly offer what I've been counseled to do, have done, or read to do. Acknowledgment of being absolutely nothing without Him has been a very good first step. Recognizing our failings and being contrite is also part of the process. We must develop a solid prayer life, yes, including that of mental prayer, but also, a devotion to the sacraments, frequenting them as often as we are able within each season of our life. We can't just settle on the obligation to attend Mass on Sundays, checking that box of the bare minimum. We should go as often as we can. This includes adoration, communion, and confession, as well. These beautiful gifts, afforded to us through the Church, are the means by which we cultivate our interior lives. If we do all of these things, we are well on our way.

There is also an immense gift found within Catholic spiritual books. We have so many amazing saints who recorded the thoughts and desires of their hearts, the events in their lives, their souls' most intimate interactions with our Lord. From the deep ocean of their words and experiences we draw an abundance of solid guidance and divine inspirations which we can apply to our own journey. St. Augustine, St. John of the Cross, St. Teresa of Avila, and St. Therese of Lisieux are just a few who have given us invaluable works from which we are able to not only learn the way of obtaining a deep interior life, but also see the inexplicable beauty and salvific ramifications in having one.

It goes without saying that we can also consider the example set by our Blessed Mother, Mary, who modeled such a beautiful and contemplative interior life as she bore, raised, and shared in the Passion of her divine son, Jesus. We should also look to St. Joseph as a model of an intense interior life. Though we don't have a lot of information about him, from what we do know, we can conjecture that his interior life had to have been deeply and intimately connected to God the Father, as well as to his foster son, Jesus, as he spent his daily life teaching Jesus, caring for Him, and keeping Him and Mary safe. From the very first visit from the angel, who told him to be not afraid to take Mary as his wife, to following the warning to flee to Egypt with his family who was in danger, St. Joseph's trust in God and his quiet servanthood speaks of the state of his interior life.

You may find yourself pausing, like I so often do, over the idea that we mothers, in our chaotic and noisy lives, could possibly find time for true contemplation and prayer, shoring up our interior life so well that it could mirror that of the saints, especially the saints whom I mention here. It is true that our ability to spend any part of the day in prayer will probably look much different than that of the saints of old who lived their life in the solitude of a hermitage, or who, at the very least, did not have a lot of children or a spouse to tend. However, we might consider the fact that we are *all* called to holiness; we are *all* called to be saints, and in order to be such, our interior life is of utmost importance. Remember that we find God in the whisper of a gentle breeze, and we risk missing His voice if we don't find time to listen in the silence. God makes saints of people from all walks of life and He will make us as holy as He desires us to be. All we have to do is be willing to give Him everything. One of my favorite aspirations to say throughout the day to aid me in this is, *"Oh Jesus, be my All; I will be entirely Thine."*

Also important, is the idea that we should never be satisfied with the state of our interior life, our relationship with the Lord. He made us with an inherent longing for Him, the depths of which we can only begin to tap here below. Therefore, we should strive continuously to cultivate our relationship, obtain as much grace as we can, and never stop pursuing Him. A long time ago, while speaking with someone about their relationship with God, they said to me, *"I'm good where I am."* I wish I had said to that person what I'm saying now. I wish I could go back and say, "Saying you're good now, at your young age and with your whole life stretching out before you, is like seeing, or at least knowing, there is, in the far distance, the most beautiful and valuable prize. But instead of doing whatever you can to reach it, you sit down on a cozy couch, and say, 'Eh, no thanks,' because you feel comfortable. Or maybe you are too lazy to make the effort. Or maybe because you don't understand what lies ahead. If we keep going, God will always continue to hand us some of the most beautiful gifts to prepare us to receive the most precious of them all: eternity with Him. Don't ever stop!" He will never stop pursuing us either, and if we look at all the ways - small and large - our lives, especially as mothers, speak to this truth, we can be sure of it.

In cultivating an interior life rooted in Christ, we are deepening our trust and faith in God's plan for us as mothers. We are opening ourselves up to being able to easily and consistently say yes to whatever He asks of us, no matter our circumstance. We are drawing closer to Jesus there on the Cross, and joyfully proclaiming our own crosses as gifts from Him, and gifts *for* Him. By abandoning ourselves in our interior connection to Him, we are allowing His grace to transform us - purified by His love - into souls bound for the Beatific Vision. And that, dear mama, is what our vocation - this, our longest labor - is really all about.

A Final Note of Love

Dear mama, I want to end this book by conveying my hope and prayer for you. This book, while my story specifically, actually belongs to God. It's His story. He is the Hero, the Alpha and the Omega. It is about Him, His love, and His grace. Nothing of the last seventeen-plus years has been about me, my children, or our large, busy family, so much as it has been about how the love of God transforms every human soul who seeks Him. We are not special in this; His love is there for every one of His children to possess.

Families like ours *are* special in that we have so many opportunities to chase that love, grab a hold of it, and be completely encompassed by it. With each new babe we welcome into our life, our opportunity starts anew. The long years of each childhood, multiplied by the number of children we have, offers such a wealth of opportunity, over and over again. Day by day. Year by year. If we turn to Him, He will meet us in every joy and sorrow we encounter, offering us an abundance of His transformative love. All we have to do is accept it.

A quick nod to another story, which, like the story of my husband and me, is part of a bigger picture, and the majority of it is for another time: Long ago, when my husband and I were searching for a new home with land to grow our landscaping business, we came across a beautiful farmhouse on twelve acres. But I knew it wasn't meant for us. My anxiety grew with every second we spent there, looking around and falling in love with it. Just as I was about to fall to pieces, I looked down and discovered a love note from God, stamped into the concrete of the backyard pool: *"Jeremiah 29:11."* If you aren't familiar with this verse, it reads, *'For I know well the plans I have in mind for you, plans for your welfare and not for woe, so as to give you a future of hope.'* This verse has always been one of my favorites, and it was exactly what I needed to see in that moment. Since that day, I have clung to the promise therein ever more. The Lord has plans for each one of us. They are for our good, for the purposes of drawing us close to Him so we may live with Him for all eternity. No matter what happens, remember this and rest in Him.

I remember kneeling at the altar rail at Mass one day, and as I gazed upon the golden Tabernacle, anticipating and longing for the Beloved, I prayed in my heart a question - *'Why, Lord, did You not call me to religious life, so I could be near to You like this more often?'* I then heard in my heart, *"You were made to be a mother."* This isn't to say I can't be near Him more often as a mother, but the fact that religious life does afford that opportunity to a greater extent is undeniable. As mothers, we face so many challenges, and while we can strive to make it more often to Mass to be closer to our Lord, the truth is that it isn't always possible due to the dynamics of our family life. But He does have a plan for our lives. Within that plan, He gives us ample opportunity to both be near to Him, and to follow the call of our vocation. Indeed, we were made to be mothers.

My prayer for you is this: May you continue your life open to God's will for it, open to whatever number of babies He wishes to send you, be that two, six, twelve (or more!), and open to the plans He has laid out for you, regardless of the pains you may endure. Embrace your cross with courage, ignoring the blaring voices coming from others, or those within your own mind, which speak of fear and inability. Trust in your intuition, which He gave to you in His perfect design, as a woman who was made to be a mother. Above all, trust in God's providence, in His divine mercy, and most especially in the transforming and saving graces found in His perfect abiding love. May Christ's peace reign in your hearts and in your homes, and may the Blessed Mother keep you within her mantle, guiding you always to the Sacred Heart of her beloved Son.

Gratitude

It is with heartfelt gratitude that I wish to acknowledge the following people, who, in various ways, have contributed to this work. Some have contributed with their prayers and encouragement. Some simply with their inspiration - both in the way they live out their vocation of motherhood and in the wisdom they've imparted to me. Some with their love and friendship, and some in a very practical way - with their time and talents. In many ways, and because of who they are, I would not be who I am without them, and this work would still be buried in the files on my laptop.

First, I cannot express the measure of gratitude I have toward my husband, Joseph, for being my partner in my own longest labor, as well as for encouraging me in my writing, in order that I may glorify God.

I am truly grateful to all my friends, especially these moms of many:

Erinn, Gwen, Loretta, Katie F., Kristy, Maria, Shelly, Anna, and Dawn. They have all been beautiful examples of trusting God to plan their families, and I have been immensely blessed to know them.

A very special thanks to the following:

My own mother, Patricia, a mother of seven, who taught me how to love God through my vocation of wife and mother, and has always encouraged me to put my trust in Him. Her perseverance and quiet strength has truly been an inspiration. Her unconditional love has given me the foundation in learning how to love my own family.

Ruth, a mother of four, who has been a second mom to me since we met thirteen years ago, who has always supported me in my vocation, and who, together with her husband, Art, has been a beautiful example of perseverance in faith, long-suffering, love and devotion, to me and my husband.

Judy, a mother of ten, who has been so instrumental on my path to letting go and letting God take control; who has encouraged me to view my marriage and motherhood through the lens of God's abundant grace and mercy. Her friendship and spiritual motherhood over the many years we've known each other has given me strength for the journey.

Debora, a mother of three, who has been like a sister to me, encouraging me and teaching me how to deepen my love of Christ and the Church, reminding me constantly that all will be well, especially when we entrust everything to Our Lady to bring to the foot of the Cross.

Ann, a mother of four, who has also been like a sister to me, and lovingly encouraged the process with this book, patiently listening to my ramblings and offering practical advice. She has been a beautiful example of mothering, as well as one of my biggest cheerleaders and strong supporters over the past few years.

Katie M., a mother of five, whose friendship over the years has been a tremendous blessing to me, and whose humility and realness in both welcoming babies and losing them, has inspired me to draw closer to Christ in my vocation, and especially in my own losses.

Leila, a mother of eight, who, despite her very busy life of being a wife and mother, as well as writing/editing her own books and standing as a pillar of Truth in the greater Catholic community, has taken the time to give me advice - both spiritual and practical, and has encouraged my efforts to be a support to others, all with the focus of bringing glory to God.

Stephanie, a mother of ten, who, aside from being a wonderful example of trusting and loving God in her vocation of wife and mother, generously agreed to lend her time and talents to the success of this work, despite her own very busy and full life as a mother to many.

Rachel, a beautiful young soul, for agreeing to be part of the practical side of this endeavor, using the gifts and talents the Lord has given her to create beautiful cover art.

Last, but certainly not least, two of my sisters, Kate and Mary, who inspire me every day with their perseverance in their vocation of motherhood and in their love of the Lord, and who have been willing vessels through which the Lord has worked tangibly in my life and the lives of others.

www.ingramcontent.com/pod-product-compliance
Lightning Source LLC
LaVergne TN
LVHW010620100826
845148LV00014B/3042

* 9 7 8 0 5 7 8 3 8 1 7 8 7 *